Fishermen's Handbook

by
Rube Allyn

GREAT OUTDOORS
PUBLISHING CO.
4747 TWENTY-EIGHTH STREET NORTH
ST. PETERSBURG, FLORIDA 33714

International Standard Book No. 8200-0103-1

Printed in the United States of America by
GREAT OUTDOORS PUBLISHING CO.
4747-28th Street North
St. Petersburg, Florida 33714

Foreword ooo

Florida is a land flowing with milk and honey for the fisherman. There are so many miles of fishing waters that it would almost be an impossibility in one's lifetime to fish all the entrancing spots.

Fishing in the State of Florida is not dulled by sameness. The coastal rivers offer a different type of fish, many the same in physical appearance, but entirely different in feeding and striking habits.

Within this book are contained highlights of 43 years of earnest pursuit of fishing for dogged and determined gamefish. All may not agree with my theories as set forth — but this is the way I found them to be.

You trout fishermen who plan retirement in our great state are lucky indeed. A wet or dry fly settling on Florida waters will give you the same thrill you have experienced with your beloved northern trout.

Contents

WORLD RECORD GAMEFISH

SPECIES	WT.	PLACE	DATE
ALBACORE *Thunnus alalunga*	88 lbs., 2 oz.	Canaria, Canary Islands	Nov. 19 1977
AMBERJACK, greater *Seriola dumerili*	149 lbs.	Bermuda	June 21, 1964
BARRACUDA, great *Sphyraena barracuda*	83 lbs.	Lagos, Nigeria	Jan. 13, 1952
BASS, giant sea *Stereolepis gigas*	563 lbs., 8 oz.	Anacapa Isl., California	Aug. 20, 1968
BASS, striped *Morone saxatilis*	72 lbs.	Cuttyhunk, Massachusetts	Oct. 10, 1969
BLUEFISH *Pomatomus saltatrix*	31 lbs., 12 oz.	Hatteras North Carolina	Jan. 30, 1972
BONEFISH *Albula vulpes*	19 lbs.	Zululand, South Africa	May 26, 1962
BONITO, Atlantic *Sarda sarda*	13 lbs., 8 oz.	Machico, Madeira Isl.	June 6, 1980
COBIA *Rachycentron canadum*	110 lbs., 5 oz.	Mombasa, Kenya	Sept. 8, 1964
DOLPHIN *Coryphaena hippurus*	87 lbs.	Papagallo Gulf, Costa Rica	Sept. 25, 1976
DRUM, black *Pogonias cromis*	113 lbs., 1 oz.	Lewes, Delaware	Sept. 15, 1975
JEWFISH *Epinephelus itajara*	680 lbs.	Fernandina Bch., Florida	May 20, 1961
MARLIN, black *Makaira indica*	1560 lbs.	Cabo Blanco, Peru	Aug. 4, 1953
MARLIN, blue (Atl.) *Makaira nigricans*	1282 lbs.	St. Thomas, Virgin Islands	Aug. 6, 1977
MARLIN, blue (Pac.) *Makaira nigricans*	1153 lbs.	Ritidian Point, Guam	Aug. 21, 1969
MARLIN, striped *Tetrapturus audax*	417 lbs., 8 oz.	Cavalli Island, New Zealand	Jan. 14, 1977
MARLIN, white *Tetrapturus albidus*	181 lbs., 14 oz.	Vitoria, Brazil	Dec. 8, 1979
PERMIT *Trachinotus falcatus*	51 lbs., 8 oz.	Lake Worth, Florida	Apr. 28, 1978
POLLOCK *Pollachius virens*	46 lbs., 7 oz.	Brielle, New Jersey	May 26, 1975
ROOSTERFISH *Nematistius pectoralis*	114 lbs.	La Paz, Baja, Mexico	June 1, 1960
SAILFISH, Atlantic *Istiophorus platypterus*	128 lbs., 1 oz.	Luanda, Angola	Mar. 27, 1974
SAILFISH, Pacific *Istiophorus platypterus*	221 lbs.	Santa Cruz Island, Ecuador	Feb. 12, 1947
SEATROUT, spotted *Cynoscion nebulosus*	16 lbs.	Mason's Beach, Virginia	May 28, 1977
SHARK, blue *Prionace glauca*	437 lbs.	Catherine Bay, N.S.W., Australia	Oct. 2, 1976
SHARK, hammerhead *Sphyrna spp.*	717 lbs.	Jacksonville Bch., Florida	July 27, 1980
SHARK, mako *Isurus spp.*	1080 lbs.	Montauk, New York	Aug. 26, 1979
SNOOK *Centropomus undecimalis*	53 lbs., 10 oz.	Rio de Parasmina, Costa Rica	Oct. 18, 1978
SWORDFISH *Xiphias gladius*	1182 lbs.	Iquique, Chile	May 7, 1953
TARPON *Megalops atlanticus*	283 lbs.	Lake Maracaibo, Venezuela	Mar. 19, 1956
TUNA, bigeye (Atl.) *Thunnus obesus*	375 lbs., 8 oz.	Ocean City, Maryland	Aug. 26, 1977
TUNA, blackfin *Thunnus atlanticus*	42 lbs.	Bermuda	June 2, 1978
TUNA, bluefin *Thunnus thynnus*	1496 lbs.	Aulds Cove, Nova Scotia, Canada	Oct. 26, 1979
WAHOO *Acanthocybium solandri*	149 lbs.	Cat Cay, Bahamas	June 15, 1962
WEAKFISH *Cynoscion regalis*	17 lbs., 14 oz.	Rye, New York	May 31, 1980
YELLOWTAIL, southern *Seriola lalandi lalandi*	111 lbs.	Bay of Islands, New Zealand	June 11, 1961

5

The Principle of Fishing

IT IS NOT necessary to say here that all of us have a desire to fish. This is instinct. Our textbooks tell us there are three great instincts which form the triangle cornerstone of existence. The desire to eat, the desire to reproduce and the desire to remain alive. For fish and animals, finding food absorbs three-quarters of the time. To eat, it is first necessary to catch the food. Whether caught alive or by some mightier being, it matters not in our studies. We, like all animals, still have that desire to catch something we can eat.

Rebel against nature if you will, suffer the taunts of neighbors, wince under a spouse's tirade on fishy clothes and funny friends, but you cannot kill intuition. It is as much a part of your life as getting married or being buried. Therefore, what we cannot destroy, let us live with, to the greatest possible enjoyment, if we must fish — and we certainly must.

To satisfy that desire we'll continue to follow the easiest course — do the thing which comes naturally. Use natural impulses of fish we wish to catch, to our advantage. We know they like to eat and to reproduce. By watching our chance we can catch the finny fellows in weak moments.

Eating time would naturally coincide with daylight and dark. Whether or not a fish is nocturnal, it is certain he is going to look for food when daylight changes on the water. This then means we should plan our fishing as close to change from night to day as possible. By that same calculation, poorest time to fish would be high noon or midnight. It's the most important point in fishing, more so than tide or bait.

Second great impulse of fish — to spawn — is a time of life when neither time, tide, nor bait makes any difference. No matter what you might throw into a school of spawning fish, they will strike it viciously. Fish spawn once a year, and it takes knowledge of their habits to find the place where this occurs. Whenever you see a school of milling fish, it will not matter what time of day or what your bait, you will have action. That's the second law of nature.

Movement of the tide stirs activity upon the ocean's floor. Hungry fish know it and they play the tides just as a poker player figures odds. Because it is natural for any creature to feel anticipation when expectation of food is very near, that nervous fish looking toward the tidal flow for food, will jump the gun and snatch at a well-presented bait just at the change of tide. Therefore, the change and first hour of tidal flow will be the best fishing time.

The Principle of Fishing

Fish can feel the coming of bad weather. Change in pressure is as noticeable in the water as in the air. It is the natural impulse of all living things to grab a bite of food when a long fasting period is expected. A spell of bad weather means this to the fish. They seek deep holes away from feeding grounds because riled water stirs up silt, and this gets in their gills and is uncomfortable. Also they do not wish to be tumbled on a beach by breakers, so they hibernate.

During bad weather fishing is poor, but just before bad weather when air pressure is declining, fish bite best. Just after a storm that has lasted several days, fish will be hungry again and they bite well. Lucky the fisherman who has a well-protected lee fishing hole, which fish might use for hibernation. He can catch fish when the storm is bad if he fishes in the morning.

Therefore, best weather condition is just before or right after a storm, or on the rising or falling of the barometer. Falling is best ordinarily, but if the storm is of long duration, the rising barometer will be best.

A slight wind, to ruffle the water and hide tackle to which the bait is attached, is ideal. A heavy wind is poor and too heavy, no good at all. A slick calm is very poor, except in the rare cases of fish which are spawning. Tarpon are a good example of this. Nothing which pertains to weather has greater influence than the spawning of fish. Best wind conditions is a moderate wind and the direction is immaterial, except as it applies to local topography, of lee or exposed fishing grounds.

Temperature of water is a rather important part of fishing calculations. All fish are so constructed and equipped to thrive best in certain water temperatures. When the water changes to a high or low above or below the naturally desired temperature range, fish will seek water more comfortable.

Fish suffer when subjected to low temperatures, and they die if trapped in shallow water where the sun heats the water to extreme heights. So the tendency of fish is to seek deeper water in cold weather, away from the chilled surface waters, or shallow waters in Spring weather changes and medium depths in mid-Summer.

A quick cold snap will cause fish to seek deep dredged holes near the shore in salt water or the swash channels in fresh water. In Spring, they will fan out over the shallow flats as the Spring sun warms the water. In mid-Summer, they will seek deeper feeding grounds, still on open bays where temperatures are near normal.

Rain, as a weather condition, has little effect on fishing, except as it accompanies wind or makes it uncomfortable for us. There is one condition in which rain has an advantage. If you are fishing on a comparatively calm day and the rain starts to ruffle the water, your chances of catching fish are greatly increased by the disturbance of the water surface which hides you. In the case of fresh water or stream fishing, the anticipation that bugs will be washed down into the water creates interest.

We have just one problem to add in our studies, the quantity of food present in the water when we intend to fish. In salt water when the bait fish have had a big spawn and are very thick on the water, fishing will not be so good. A well-fed Mackerel is not hungry. The same applies to fresh water. When heavy rains have washed a myriad of bugs and insects into the water, the Bass will not bite well, they are not hungry.

So now, students, let's see how we have progressed on our fishing lessons:

We must know exactly the time of tide change at the place we wish to fish, and try to select the spot with the change closest to our best time of day.

If we are lucky enough to catch the barometer going up or down, we add this advantage to time and tide.

We know that extreme temperatures vitally affect fish, and we add water temperature to our calculations in deciding what kind of fish to go after, and how deep to fish.

The Tides

THE RULES of tidal flow throughout the world, are that: "The tide shall ebb and flow twice in 24 hours with the change coming each day, 50 minutes later." Like all rules, this is general . . . . It is true for the world as a whole, but the Gulf of Mexico is just one of the many exceptions to that rule and, incidentally, the greatest.

The tide is affected by the moon. As the moon rises in the heavens, so does the tide. As the moon declines, so does the tide go out. When the moon is full, the tide is stronger; when it is in first or last quarter, the tide is weaker. This is because the sun also has some tide control as well as the moon.

So we can put it like this: The moon, traveling in an irregular path across the heavens, passes from one side to the other of the Equator. When farthest away on either side, the tide is stronger, because it has less competition from the sun.

Therefore, when the sun works farther south in the Winter, the moon has the best time of it on the North side, so the tides in Winter are extremely low. In the Summer when the sun is North, the moon does its best work on the South side and the tides are extremely high.

The high tides of early Summer are strong full tides. They are called "Spring tides."

The little half tides which occur when the moon is on the Equator, are called "Neap" tides. The origin of this word is uncertain, but this writer believes it comes from the saying of old New England settlers: "The tide today will be no higher than a wagon neap." A wagon neap is the wagon tongue or pole. That would indicate a small rise, especially on coastal areas like New England where the tide rise and fall is extremely great.

Rise and fall of the tide varies greatly with locality. Least amount of rise and fall is in the Gulf of Mexico with Tampa Bay having that honor. Officially the tide is only supposed to move 12 inches in Tampa Bay. On the upper bay, it seldom moves that much. This is comparable to an average movement of 40 feet on the Bay of Fundy in the Far North.

While the range of the tide through most all the world is semidiurnal (two high and two low tides a day), in the Tampa Bay area it is mostly diurnal, or one high and low tide a day. The official tables give many semidiurnal days, but on these days, movement is often less than one-tenth of a foot.

The two greatest factors exclusive of the moon which affect tide movement are wind and barometer. When the wind is out of the South, the tides will be higher than expected, and may not go out.

When the barometer is low, the tides will be high, regardless of what the moon is doing. In fact, a fast-dropping barometer will take the operation of tides right out of Lunar control. The lower the glass, the higher comes the water. The reverse is also true. When the barometer is high, then the water disappears, the tide goes out. An exceptionally high glass can take over from Lunar control.

This may be explained by comparing it to a rubber bulb filled with water. When you apply pressure, which is a high barometer, the water is squeezed out. When the pressure is released, the water is sucked in. Thus, with the lowering of barometric pressure, water is sucked up to wherever the pressure is lowest.

A study of the tide tables will show the irregular tidal movement from day to day, both in number of tides and volume of water flow. The moon, greatest force affecting the tides, loses its pull when it crosses the Equator, which is twice a month on the average. The pull increases as the moon travels to the maximum North or South declination.

So, there you have the tides in capsule form. This information may not make you a tide expert, but there should be enough dope here to explain that question: "What's the matter with the tide today? It didn't come in!"

BAROMETER

THE OLD SAYING: "When the wind blows from the south, it blows bait in the fishes' mouth; when from the east, the fishing is least." The man who catches no fish on an east wind probably doesn't fish when an east wind is blowing.

Early morning and late afternoon will produce more strikes than any other time. Night fishing, however, cannot be completely ignored. If you do fish in the dark, tie on a Jitterbug. Slowly retrieve the self-acting plug across the surface and you'll get action.

A rippled bay or stream is to be preferred to a flat, glassy calm — especially where top water lures are being used.

The study of weather, moon phases, water temperature, and such things, is very interesting in its application to fishing. The John Alden Knight Solunar Tables are quite helpful to anyone who wants to pursue this subject.

The density of light has a bearing on fishing. Early morning and late afternoon is the most productive time of the day as a rule. Fish favor subdued light conditions for feeding.

FALLING BAROMETER

31 to 30.8	Fair and cool, variable winds.
30.8 to 30.5	Fair and warmer, followed by wind and rain after one or two days.
30.5 to 30.2	Storm developing in the direction toward which the wind is blowing.
30.2 to 29.9	Cloudy and warmer, with unsettled weather and rain.
29.9 to 29.6	Unsettled weather, increasing winds and warmer.
29.6 to 29.3	Clearing. Slight squalls. Fair and warmer tomorrow.
29.3 to 29.0	Clearing weather with high winds, accompanied by squalls and cooler.
29.0 to 28.7	Stormy weather.

RISING BAROMETER

29. to 29.3	Clearing with high winds and cool wave.
29.3 to 29.6	High winds with cool wave preceded by squalls.
29.6 to 29.9	Fair weather with fresh winds tonight and tomorrow.
29.9 to 30.2	Fair with brisk winds which will diminish.
30.2 to 30.5	Generally fair weather, probably cool today with variable winds.
30.5 to 30.8	Clear weather tonight and continued cool with moderate winds.
30.8 to 31.0	Southeast rains with high winds.

WEATHER

At selected locations in and near boating areas, storm warnings are displayed by flag hoists or lights. Display points are usually Coast Guard Stations, yacht marinas, or municipal piers. A boatman should become familiar with the display stations in his area and the meanings of the signals.

Don't ignore a Small Craft Warning. Remember, too, that you can encounter bad weather, even with a fair forecast and no storm signals flying. For example, thunderstorms and squalls are often unpredictable, yet they can be very dangerous.

STORM SIGNALS

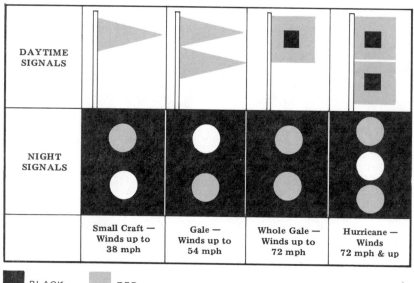

	Small Craft — Winds up to 38 mph	Gale — Winds up to 54 mph	Whole Gale — Winds up to 72 mph	Hurricane — Winds 72 mph & up
DAYTIME SIGNALS				
NIGHT SIGNALS				

BLACK   RED

As an aid to the boatman in getting weather information, the U.S. Weather Bureau publishes COASTAL WARNING FACILITIES CHARTS for local areas on the Atlantic, Pacific, and Gulf coasts, as well as the Great Lakes, Puerto Rico, and Hawaii. These charts give the location and telephone numbers of all Weather Bureau Offices, the location and schedules of all AM, FM, and TV stations that broadcast marine weather information, weather schedules of marine radio telephone stations and air navigation radio stations. The location of all storm warning display stations, with an explanation of their meanings, are also shown. These charts are obtained by writing the Superintendent of Documents, U.S. Government Printing Office, Washington, D.C. 20401, and stating the local area desired. Each chart costs ten cents.

How To Get There

AT NIGHT the stars guide you. The Big Dipper has three stars in the handle, which are well defined — and four in the "cup." The lower two will line up with the star off to the North, known as Polaris or North Star. By facing North, you can select other stars for bearings on East and South: Always remember that when facing North, your right hand points East.

This is the way to place a watch and a match for use as a compass. In this case, the shadow is falling across the figure 8, which would indicate that South was at approximately 9:30, North at 3:30; East at 6:30; and West at 12:30. To get your bearings at sea, lay the watch flat on a seat or, if it is rough, hold it in the palm of your hand. Take a matchstick or anything which will stand 2 inches or more high vertically.

This upright is placed alongside the watch at the edge so a shadow is thrown across the face. Now turn the watch until the shadow lies along the hour hand, just covering it exactly.

With a shadow on the hour hand, notice the distance between this and the numeral 12 at the top of the watch. Exactly in the center, between 12 and the shadow, will be the direction South. North is in the opposite direction, and East is on the left FACING SOUTH, or right, FACING NORTH. West is opposite East.

If the time is Noon, the shadow will fall along the hour hand and the figure 12 at the same time, so this is South, with calculations, thus the figure 9 would be East and 3 would be West.

At night, your best and most accurate guide is Polaris, the North Star. This star can be located by observing the well-defined star cluster known as the "Big Dipper."

Notice that two stars in the cup of Big Dipper are in line, which imaginary line can be drawn with the eye to bring Polaris into direct line also. In other words, two stars on the bottom of the Big Dipper line up with themselves and Polaris.

It would be wise to practice this observation in the back yard a few times if you plan to do any night fishing. Or it is a smart thing to get it fixed in your mind just in case you find yourself doing some unintentional night cruising.

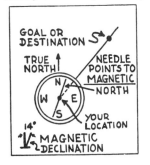

If you are a stranger to the fishing grounds, the fastest way to get there is to buy a fishing map of the locality in which you wish to fish.

You should know the magnetic declination (deviation) of the compass from true, geographical North for travel by map and compass. (Geological maps show the declination to allow.)

Find true North by compass. Then spread the map flat and lay the compass on so the top is toward true North. Find your location and draw a line to goal. Lay compass over your location on map to find compass reading in degrees to follow.

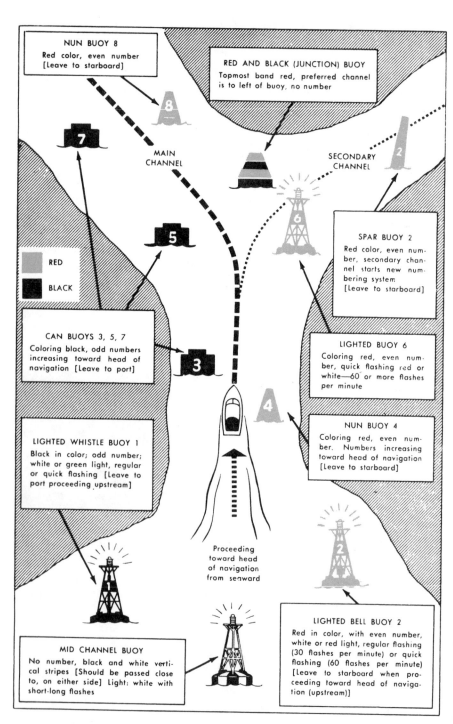

NUN BUOY 8
Red color, even number [Leave to starboard]

RED AND BLACK (JUNCTION) BUOY
Topmost band red, preferred channel is to left of buoy, no number

MAIN CHANNEL

SECONDARY CHANNEL

SPAR BUOY 2
Red color, even number, secondary channel starts new numbering system [Leave to starboard]

RED

BLACK

CAN BUOYS 3, 5, 7
Coloring black, odd numbers increasing toward head of navigation [Leave to port]

LIGHTED BUOY 6
Coloring red, even number, quick flashing red or white—60 or more flashes per minute

LIGHTED WHISTLE BUOY 1
Black in color; odd number; white or green light, regular or quick flashing [Leave to port proceeding upstream]

NUN BUOY 4
Coloring red, even number. Numbers increasing toward head of navigation [Leave to starboard]

Proceeding toward head of navigation from seaward

MID CHANNEL BUOY
No number, black and white vertical stripes [Should be passed close to, on either side] Light: white with short-long flashes

LIGHTED BELL BUOY 2
Red in color, with even number, white or red light, regular flashing (30 flashes per minute) or quick flashing (60 flashes per minute) [Leave to starboard when proceeding toward head of navigation (upstream)]

12

Locating the Fishing Grounds

FIRST THING you need to learn about fishing is where you plan to do it. On the surface, the water everywhere looks about the same, but underneath there is a vast difference. Nine-tenths of the bottom in bay, lake, or river, is unproductive fishing. That magical one-tenth is where you must cast your bait.

Quickest way to get started in salt-water fishing is to hire a professional guide to teach you the fundamentals. With this handbook you can refresh your memory on all the points learned this way. Most important is to get an idea of where you're going.

When your guide stops at that "Glory Hole," the swash channel or eel-grass bttom where Trout lurk, far removed from shore, make certain that you can return if the drop is productive. Pick out a landmark on shore, imagine a line running through the boat to the opposite shore. Tie it in. Pick out a point at right angles and tie that in with an object on the opposite shore.

While you have it in mind, mark this on your fishing map — a copy of which will become the most important part of your equipment. Next time you pass this way in your own boat, you have but to follow either of the lines until the right-angle landmark lines up — and then you have it.

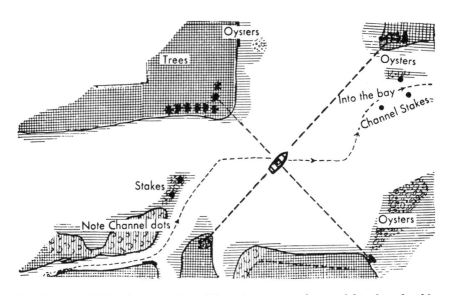

Boat keel should lie along one dotted line. An oar, or other straight edge, should follow second line. Angles at crossing are 90 degrees.

Sea Trout prefer open water and grass bottom; Sheepshead like barnacle-encrusted old wrecks; Grouper prefer rocky bottom; and Mackerel are free swimmers, most plentiful in open passes between bay and sea. Larger fish, such as Cobia, Barracuda, and Kings, will be found in deep water near a sea buoy, or where rock formation on the bottom offers adequate hiding places for small fish.

Once you have located the "Glory Hole" (which will become your standby for months or years to come), you're ready for the next step on the fishing trail of happy holidays.

How to Anchor Your Boat

IT IS IMPORTANT to anchor your boat correctly when you have located the fishing grounds. Proper use of ground tackle can make the difference between a successful day's fishing and just ordinary luck. Fish are sensitive to sound and shadows, so these things must be taken into consideration.

Best procedure would be to drift or slow troll over the area where you intend to fish. When activity is encountered — either a good solid strike or a catch — carefully note the locality. While the fish is still on your line, slip the anchor over quietly so the current or tide will hold you in position to cast against the sun if possible. The shadow of your boat will be thrown in the opposite direction from where the fish are believed to be located.

Once settled, a steady concentration of Chum can be tossed over, to drift down on the fishing area. Wounded sardines or broken pieces of shrimp make good Chum. Any kind of fish scraps is worthwhile to draw cruising fish from the surrounding area.

If you are using artificial bait, it is best to continue drifting and casting, dropping your lure in new areas with each cast, unless you have located a school of Blues, Mackerel, or Channel Bass. Then anchoring is the ticket!

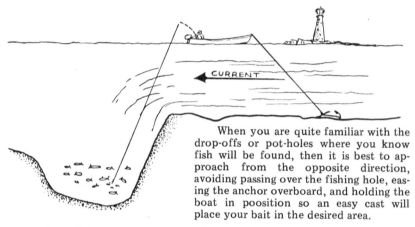

When you are quite familiar with the drop-offs or pot-holes where you know fish will be found, then it is best to approach from the opposite direction, avoiding passing over the fishing hole, easing the anchor overboard, and holding the boat in poosition so an easy cast will place your bait in the desired area.

Sometimes it is advantageous to anchor with a bridle when three persons are fishing. In this way the boat will be held in a sidewise position to allow more freedom — and casting room. Such a bridle can be rigged before you start, and the anchor line attached as you stop to fish.

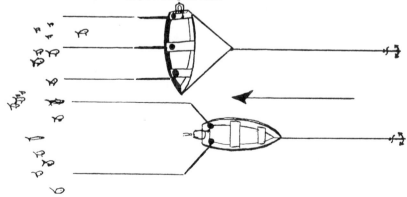

Tying the Lines and Leaders

Strain of the line will be equally distributed in the six loops so that at no point will line cut line.

More than 75% of lost fish due to broken lines is caused by improperly tying the line to swivel when rigging fishing tackle. Greatest strain between reel and fish comes at this point, which, if applied to one particular portion of the line where it is in contact with the swivel, will break at considerably less than the breaking test the manufacturer guarantees.

Important point is the knot, demonstrated on this page.

It is wise to take loops through the swivel, then insert two fingers in the loop. Twist the loose end around the taut line at least six times. Pull the loose end through the loop and give it three half-hitches on the taut side of the loop. Then pull it tight.

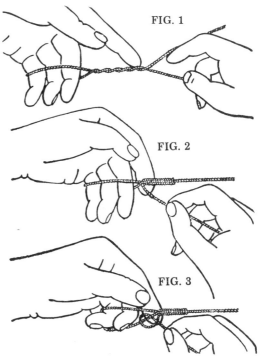

FIG. 1

FIG. 2

FIG. 3

TOP

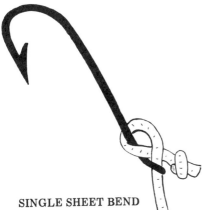

SINGLE SHEET BEND

Here's the one best tie to attach a fish hook on a line. There are others, some more complicated, but this will answer most any purpose. The Single Sheet Bend, with over-hand knot in the end of the line tie for light tackle.

Sunset Fishing Lines came up with a technique for tying its Coral King and Flexon monofilament, which was reported to test consistently at less than 3% loss. Its knot resembles the common "end loop," except that the "U" section, bent backward, is given three full wraps around its own body before the "U" inserts through the loop.

This knot admittedly is not as small as some — not a material disadvantage when monofilament is tied to leader, swivel, snelled flies, or most artificial lures and plugs.

Fishhooks You Should Know

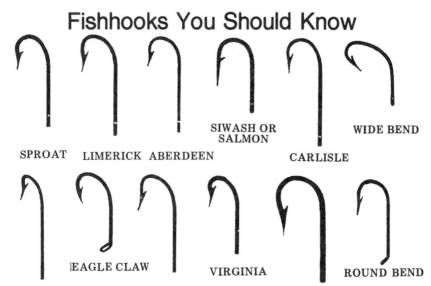

SPROAT LIMERICK ABERDEEN SIWASH OR SALMON CARLISLE WIDE BEND

CHESTERTOWN EAGLE CLAW O'SHAUGHNESSY VIRGINIA BIG GAME ROUND BEND

MOST HOOKS have medium or regular shanks for all-around fishing. Long shanks are good for Snook, Pike, or Muskies, because these fish have gill flaps which can cut a leader. Catfish, Eels, and Sucker Fish, which swallow bait, need long shank hooks. Shanks are generally straight, except those designed to hold insect lures in place.

Wherever possible, it is best to use a fine wire hook. Some spring in the shank is desirable. Heavy fish require heavy hooks, so rig according to your game, always keeping in mind that odds are with you when you keep the hook inconspicuous, using the lightest possible.

Hooks with round bends have a wide gap between the point and shank. They provide a lot of clearance and are good for large baits and fish with big mouths. Hooks with sharp-angled bends are used for fish with small mouths, those which tend to swallow the bait. Eels, for example. Hooks may be offset to snag slow-striking fish, such as Black Bass. The eyes are adjusted for use in making artificial flies or live bait. In the latter case, it's the ball eye, most popular hook pattern.

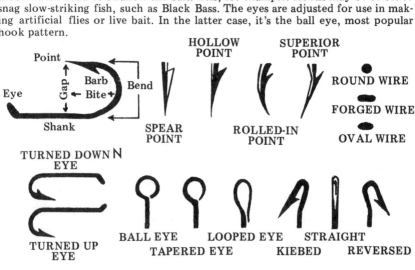

HOLLOW POINT SUPERIOR POINT ROUND WIRE FORGED WIRE OVAL WIRE

Point Barb Bend Gap Eye Bite Shank SPEAR POINT ROLLED-IN POINT

TURNED DOWN EYE TURNED UP EYE BALL EYE TAPERED EYE LOOPED EYE STRAIGHT KIEBED REVERSED

Basic fishing knots

Bait Hook Knot

FOR BAIT HOOKS without tackle and feathers, where a strong holding knot is desired, the "Double Eye" knot has been found most satisfactory after exhaustive tests at the DuPont Research Laboratories, Arlington, N.J.

FIG. 1
Tie a "Single Running" knot on the end of the leader and push it through the eye of the hook.

FIG. 2
Pass this loop over the bend of the hook and then draw it up to the eye.

FIG. 3
Take the short end of the "Single Running" knot, push it under the loop, against the shank, and draw up tight.

FIG. 4
This is what the finished knot should look like when you put a strain on the line.

Perfection Loop Knot

THE PERFECTION Loop Knot is good to use when tying a loop on the end of a nylon leader. Be sure that it is pulled up tightly and evenly for a secure knot. Test it completely to see that it will not slip.

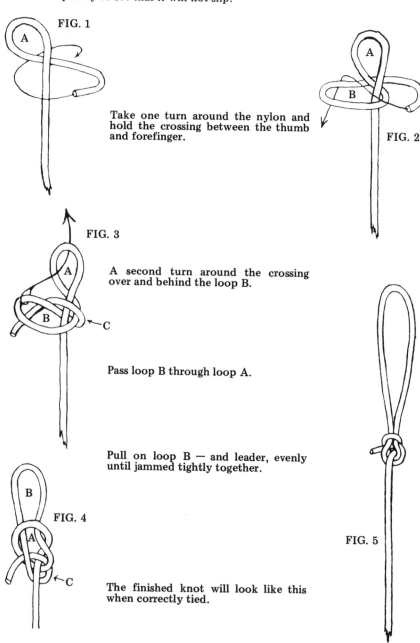

FIG. 1

Take one turn around the nylon and hold the crossing between the thumb and forefinger.

FIG. 2

FIG. 3

A second turn around the crossing over and behind the loop B.

Pass loop B through loop A.

Pull on loop B — and leader, evenly until jammed tightly together.

FIG. 4

The finished knot will look like this when correctly tied.

FIG. 5

Blood Knot

LAP THE ENDS of the strands to be joined and twist one around the other, making at least three turns. The drawing shows only three and one-half turns, to avoid complexity. Count the turns made, place the end between the strands, following the arrow.

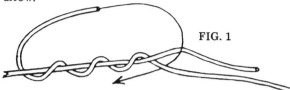

FIG. 1

Hold the end against the turns already made, between the thumb and forefinger at point marked 'X' to keep from unwinding. Now wind the other short end around the other strand for the same number of turns, but in the opposite direction.

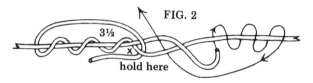

FIG. 2

This shows how the knot would look if held firmly in place. Actually, as soon as released, the turns equalize.

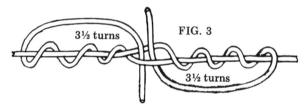

FIG. 3

And the turns look like this. Now pull on both ends of the leader.

FIG. 4

Appearance of the finished knot. All that remains to be done is to cut off the short ends close to the knot.

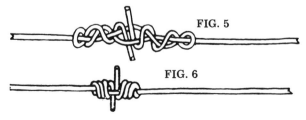

FIG. 5

FIG. 6

Dropper Knot

THIS KNOT is one used frequently on streams or lakes, and is highly recommended for use with nylon leaders. Once tied, it will hold firmly, never creeping up or down the line. The nylon leader has no strain excessive to the breaking point at one place.

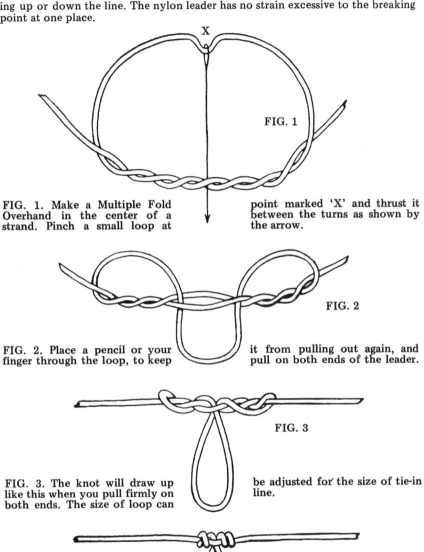

FIG. 1

FIG. 1. Make a Multiple Fold Overhand in the center of a strand. Pinch a small loop at point marked 'X' and thrust it between the turns as shown by the arrow.

FIG. 2

FIG. 2. Place a pencil or your finger through the loop, to keep it from pulling out again, and pull on both ends of the leader.

FIG. 3

FIG. 3. The knot will draw up like this when you pull firmly on both ends. The size of loop can be adjusted for the size of tie-in line.

FIG. 4

FIG. 4. Finished loop knot, which will hold as long as the nylon lasts on either side. This is an excellent knot for trot-line rigs or bottom fishing terminal tackle, using one or more drops.

20

The Return Knot

THIS KNOT is useful for tying leader to a fly or small hook. It is exceptionally strong and well adapted to nylon leaders.

FIG. 1

FIG. 1. Put the end of the leader through the eye of the hook and up in front, holding the loop end between thumb and forefinger.

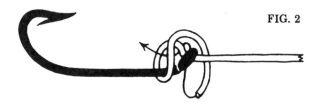

FIG. 2

FIG. 2. Make a second turn behind the first, holding open also.

FIG. 3

FIG. 3. Pass the end under both loops, and pull on the standing part of leader. As the coils draw up, be sure the loops are pushed over the eye of the hook.

FIG. 4

FIG. 4. Pull up the knot tightly and it will have the appearance as shown above. This is the neatest and probably the most secure of all hook knots.

Leader Knot

HERE ARE a few basic knots that fishermen the world over have used with good success:

X Hold Here

FIG. 1

Used for joining a leader to a line.

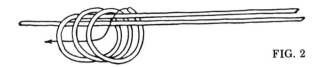

FIG. 2

Lap the ends of the strands as shown, holding with thumb and forefinger.

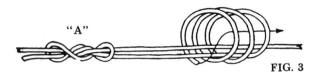

"A"

FIG. 3

Loop end around both strands three times and pull through as indicated above. Loop the other short end around the other strand in similar fashion to Fig. 2.

FIG. 4

When both sections of the knot have been pulled up, take the long ends and pull together, being careful that even pressure is exerted on the lines.

FIG. 5

The finished knot. Cut off the short ends close to the knot.

The Splice is a Sailor's Handiest Knot

FIG. 1. The size of eye is determined and the rope is unraveled. The strands are numbered for ease in identification.

FIG. 2. All strands have now been passed through the main rope. The operation is repeated 3 times for a complete splice.

A SPLICE is not hard to make, it just looks difficult to the beginner. Like a hitch or knot, it is just a matter of careful handling and remembering the turns. In reality, a splice should be taught ahead of all other ties. It is so useful and sturdy.

We'll start with an ordinary eye splice, such as is used to slip over a cleat or a tent stake. First thing is to unravel the 3 strands of the rope. If you're working with ¼-inch or less material, about 8 inches will suffice. Larger rope takes a foot. Best to use more than actually needed if you are just a beginner.

Form an eye and bend the rope so it crosses with the correct size you wish. Now choose the strand nearest to main rope (No. 1 in accompanying diagrams) and pass it under one of the main rope strands as shown in Fig. 2. To open strands, twist rope against direction of lay. If you have a fid handy, the pointed end can be inserted to open strands or to hold it from twisting. A fid is a hardwood dowel.

FIG. 3. The operation is repeated with strands 2 & 3. Always careful to work in counter-clockwise direction.

FIG. 4. This is the most important step. With both ends of bend lying together, pass No. 1 strand thru closest opening in the main strand.

Now, with eye splice pointing toward you, choose the next strand of main rope in a clockwise direction and pass No. 2 strand through it in a counter-clockwise direction. Do the same with No. 3 strand.

Now take No. 1 strand and pass it over main rope strand immediately ahead of it and under the next main rope strand in a counter-clockwise direction when viewed from the eye end of the rope (Fig. 4). Repeat this operation with No. 2 and No. 3 strands, passing them over one main rope strand and under the next and pulling them in tightly. Now you have 2 tucks in the splice, but it takes 3 to complete it, so pass all strands in turn, over one — and under one — of the main rope strands. What's left hanging can be trimmed off, not too close, but with enough to take care of any pull-in which will occur when the rope is under strain.

To make it all nice and neat, lay the rope on deck and roll it with palm of your hand until the whole is rounded up and the braided shape disappears.

This is a splice which will last as long as the rope itself and will hold when every other place breaks.

FIG. 5. This is the complete splice. Note ends of rope left for adjustment and pulling in. When splice is "rolled," the strands will match in perfectly.

Casting with Conventional Rod and Reel

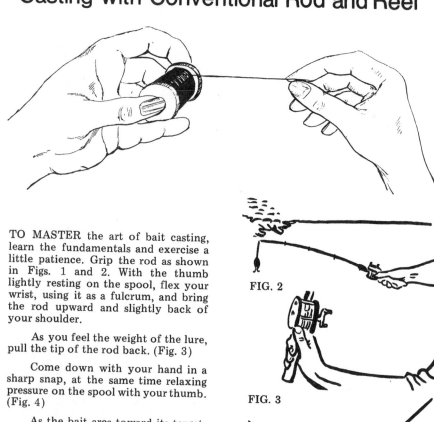

TO MASTER the art of bait casting, learn the fundamentals and exercise a little patience. Grip the rod as shown in Figs. 1 and 2. With the thumb lightly resting on the spool, flex your wrist, using it as a fulcrum, and bring the rod upward and slightly back of your shoulder.

As you feel the weight of the lure, pull the tip of the rod back. (Fig. 3)

Come down with your hand in a sharp snap, at the same time relaxing pressure on the spool with your thumb. (Fig. 4)

As the bait arcs toward its target, apply pressure ever so slightly to the running spool to avoid over-running or bad backlashing. (Fig. 5)

For reels without level-winding, the line should be evenly distributed by guiding it on the spool as you make your retrieve. (Fig. 6)

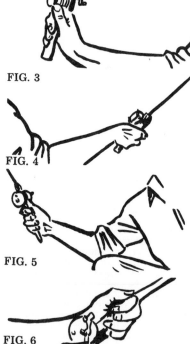

FIG. 2

FIG. 3

FIG. 4

FIG. 5

FIG. 6

FIG. 1

How to Spin Cast

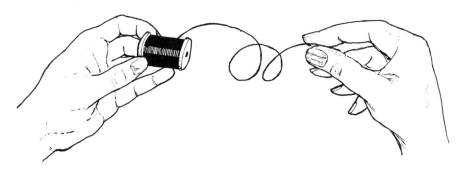

SPINNING LINE DELIVERY

SPINCASTING is probably the easiest method for the novice to master. It is also the least tiring of all the various ways to fish for Bass, with the exception of live-bait fishing. The spinning outfit is the middle of the road between fly fishing and plug casting. The tackle is light and does not lend itself well to horsing or to game fishing. To become a good spin fisherman, one must learn a little different technique than either fly rod or casting rod methods.

Grasp the rod handle, letting the upright from the reel base rest between the middle fingers. With the index finger extended, touch the spool — then, with the left hand, open the bail or pickup.

A flip with the rod will send your lure sailing. You will feel the line against the tip of your index finger as it leaves the spool.

As your lure reaches the target, it may be dropped in place by firm pressure against the spool with the index finger.

When a spinning line is cranked in with tension against it, the line will twist itself and your succeeding casts will be full of loops and snarls.

Pump the game fish in toward you by lifting the rod without cranking; then, as the rod tip is lowered, crank up the slack in the line. Repeat this until the fish is ready for netting.

Should the line become twisted, break off the lure and troll the bare line behind the outboard five to ten minutes. Most of the kinks will come out.

A spinning reel is no better than the brake that is an integral part of the reel. Adjust the brake on your reel before fishing to allow the fighting fish to run without breaking the line. When playing a stubborn fish on a spinning rod, do not crank him in against the pull of the line; if you do, you are headed for trouble.

You may use a bass bug with your spinning rod for good results. Buy one of the plastic floats or the Fli-tosser designed for your spinning line and tie your bug about three feet from the casting float or Fli-tosser. Work it slowly. Let the bug rest on the surface between jerks . . . as long as 30 seconds. This is murder for late-afternoon fishing.

Surf Casting

SURF CASTING, a type of fishing in which there is usually plenty of elbow room, is an extremely satisfying sport in several ways. The fisherman has a chance to try his skill for long casts. Ample opportunity is presented for picnics and leisure while the bait lies idle on the bottom; the wife and kids can go along without upsetting the fishing.

FIG. 1

A surf-casting rod is usually a stout 7-foot Burma or glass job, with a 200-yard reel. A 9-thread line makes for long casts and sporty fishing, although 12 to 15 would be suitable.

The idea is to lay a bait out beyond the line of surf in the swash, where shore-running fish such as Channel Bass, Bluefish, and Pompano, will be found. A good weight is needed and a light leader and hook (see guide section on rigs).

In surf casting, it is best to hold the right hand directly under the reel, with thumb resting on side of reel. The left hand grasps the butt of the rod solidly, very near the end.

The line, weight, and bait is laid out behind as you prepare for the cast, with about 10 feet of line off the reel. The cast is started by tensing your body so as to apply force, like the snapping of a steel spring.

FIG. 2

The following throw should be at arm's length, holding the rod high with the right hand well above the head, left arm applying pulling force as right hand holds back. When the bait is sailing well out over the water, lower the rod tip slowly, finally coming to a horizontal position pointing at, but slightly above, the area where the bait landed. One the bait is in, slack should be taken out of the line with a gentle reeling in until the weight is felt. The rod butt should then be placed in the belly socket if Channel Bass is the game. Most all surf running fish are attracted best by moving the bait occasionally. This tends to attract fish in the vicinity which might not have noticed it. Too much motion, however, will have the opposite effect and alarm the fish.

FIG. 3   FIG. 4

It is not a bad idea to try periods of quiet when the bait is kept motionless. This is especially true where surf Shark fishing is the sport.

Fly Casting

THE DELICATE art of fly casting for Bass is a complete study in itself. There is great satisfaction to be derived from a perfect cast to the right spot. It's sheer poetry to watch your bug or fly descend with a slight splat on the water like a spent insect, then come to life just before it disappears into the depths with a mighty swirl. The strike of the Bass is a beautiful symphony to the ear of the angler.

How to fly cast could be incorporated into an entire book. Briefly, here are a few simple steps to get you started.

Your rod is at 9 o'clock (Fig. 1).

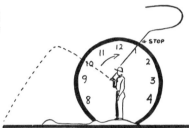

Bring it upward to 1 o'clock, as in Fig. 2. The heavy line will follow the rod tip and, as you stop the upward and backward motion of the rod, the line will uncurl itself and bring a backward pressure to the rod tip.

As this pressure is felt (Fig. 3), start your forward cast (Figs. 4 & 5).

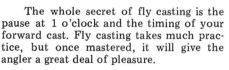

The whole secret of fly casting is the pause at 1 o'clock and the timing of your forward cast. Fly casting takes much practice, but once mastered, it will give the angler a great deal of pleasure.

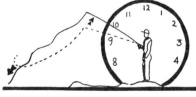

Fly fishing is the most difficult of the three methods of casting. To master this technique you must be able to lay out at least 40 feet of line. If you want results, practice. It takes practice and more practice.

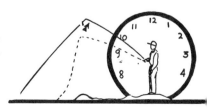

Surf Casting Rigs

SURF CASTING is always popular for both the veteran and novice fisherman, but unless the skill of the veteran is used in adjusting tackle rig, the novice will come home empty-handed.

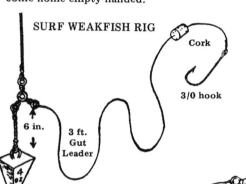

The lower illustration is a rig for Channel Bass (Redfish) for the beach. The 4-ounce pyramid sinker holds the bait out, but is loose on the line, permitting the bait to circulate. The leather thong designed to prevent rocks cutting the line is not always necessary. Also a nylon leader may be substituted for gut.

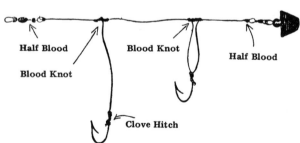

Upper illustration is the same rig designed for Sea Trout. These fish are not bottom-feeders, and appreciate the bait being held off bottom. This is accomplished by use of a cork. Nylon leader is indicated. It is wise to remember that the less weight in the sinker, the more freedom for casting. This is entirely controlled by tide pressure. Keep several sizes in your tackle box and, after testing, select the size best suited.

RIG FOR WHITING

A good rig for Whiting or small fish roving the shoreline is this nylon combination. The sinker is shaped like an inverted bell and the drops are tied in as described on another page. Drop nearest the sinker is shorter so they do not interfere. It is a good idea to put a leather thong in the rig between the leader and the line.

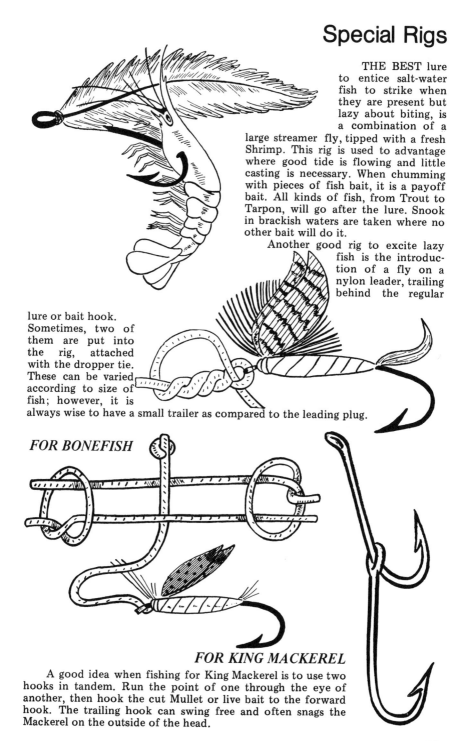

Special Rigs

THE BEST lure to entice salt-water fish to strike when they are present but lazy about biting, is a combination of a large streamer fly, tipped with a fresh Shrimp. This rig is used to advantage where good tide is flowing and little casting is necessary. When chumming with pieces of fish bait, it is a payoff bait. All kinds of fish, from Trout to Tarpon, will go after the lure. Snook in brackish waters are taken where no other bait will do it.

Another good rig to excite lazy fish is the introduction of a fly on a nylon leader, trailing behind the regular lure or bait hook. Sometimes, two of them are put into the rig, attached with the dropper tie. These can be varied according to size of fish; however, it is always wise to have a small trailer as compared to the leading plug.

FOR BONEFISH

FOR KING MACKEREL

A good idea when fishing for King Mackerel is to use two hooks in tandem. Run the point of one through the eye of another, then hook the cut Mullet or live bait to the forward hook. The trailing hook can swing free and often snags the Mackerel on the outside of the head.

Trolling Rigs

TROLLING RIGS are successful only in accordance with the time and place and the fish sought. Some conditions require fast trolling, others, slow. Some days the squid works best, others, it is the spoon or feather. Best policy is to have some of each on hand.

Generally speaking, King and Spanish Mackerel require fast trolling, four m.p.h., using artificial lures. With live Sardines or Mullet strips, the boat movement is held to a speed which just barely keeps the line taut.

ABOUT 6-ft. LEADER

Mackerel, especially when close inshore, prefer the yellow bullhead feather rig, which is trolled at four miles an hour, about twenty feet back of the boat. Be sure a good swivel is in the rig.

ABOUT 9-ft. LEADER

King Mackerel, Bonito, and deep-sea fish are partial to the cut bait trolling strip. It is important to tie your leader with the loop shown and cut the strip with a very small amount of flesh. Mullet belly is ideal.

Remove portion of backbone

15-ft. WIRE LEADER

Sailfish and other deep-sea gamefish are partial to the whole fish rig. This is a bit more difficult to make. Small Mullet or bait fish are slit open at the back and a portion of the backbone removed. The hook is inserted through the anal fin. Top of bait is then clamped shut or sewed. This is trolled slowly from 20 to 100 feet astern.

The small yellow bullhead jib is a good bait for Grouper, especially when rigged with a Mullet strip hanging from the hook. Grouper strike hard at this feather rig when presented a few feet off their rocky bottom habitat. It is best to attach a weight to the line about three feet up from the jig, heavy enough to keep the lure down. This can be determined after several tests.

12-INCH WIRE

Trolling over suspected rock bottom areas will arouse the Grouper on the first run. Usually after hooking the first fish, the anchor is let down and bottom fishing started. Experienced fishermen consider this trolling method a "fish-finding" rig. Often after several catches, the Grouper become wary and refuse to strike again. They will take still fished baits, where trolled ones are refused.

Bottom Fishing Rigs

BOTTOM FISHING from any kind of boat is best accomplished with a rig that is sensitive to feel. Two distinct types are recommended. The top illustration shows a bottom rig for fishing in fairly shallow water, especially sandy or gravel bottom. The two hooks are set at different lengths so as not to interfere with each other. This is good for Sheepshead and Flounder.

Lower illustration is a deep-sea rig, used where there is motion to the boat or in surf. The sinker pulls directly down on the line and can be increased to 2 or 3 hooks by adding 3-way swivels.

Variations of the bottom fishing rig can be worked out by increasing the length of line between the sinker and the 3-way swivel. Where the bottom is rocky or heavy with grass, this rig is not nearly as satisfactory as on a smooth or gravel bed. The tide also has much to do with efficiency. Size of the sinker can be increased or decreased to meet these conditions.

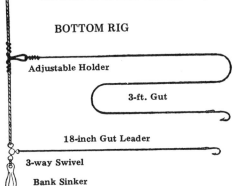

BOTTOM RIG

Adjustable Holder

3-ft. Gut

18-inch Gut Leader

3-way Swivel

Bank Sinker

CHANNEL BASS

When the Reds come charging along the coast, it's time for a good rig that will hold a fair-sized bait and attract the fish. The idea is to have a surf sinker that will stay put and a long wire leader which can be expected to sway around in the surf. The double gang hook is designed to hold a small Mullet or Squid — anything that can be extended to make a larger bait. This rig is good for Stripers, too, and in the heavier models, is a good Channel Bass outfit.

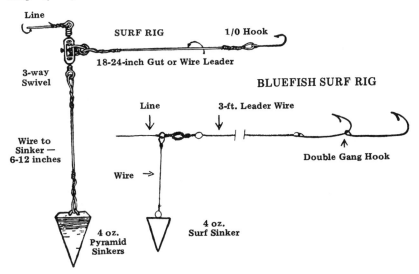

Line

SURF RIG   1/0 Hook

18-24-inch Gut or Wire Leader

3-way Swivel

BLUEFISH SURF RIG

Line   3-ft. Leader Wire

Wire to Sinker — 6-12 inches

Wire →

Double Gang Hook

4 oz. Pyramid Sinkers

4 oz. Surf Sinker

Casting and Trolling

TOP-WATER casting with live bait calls for a sliding cork rig. The hook, preferably a No. 4 Carlisle, is secured on a nylon leader 30 inches long. This is tied to a small swivel. On the line is placed a wooden "button." Then the line is threaded through the cork and tied to the swivel. Pinch-on leads are used for the amount of weight needed. When the depth of water is determined, the button is "stopped" on the line. The button then stops the cork at the proper depth. In casting, it slides to the weights. If the cork appears to jam on the weights, another button should be added ahead of them.

Top Rig for Fly-fishing: Using live bait or particularly active bait fished near the surface or in a strong tide, it is best to hook a small pinch-on weight ahead of the swivel. Then use 3 feet or more of nylon leader. This is for small Tarpon, Snook, or Permit, when fishing in a tide.

When casting and trolling, a Feather Dude is a simpler rig. The Dude is hooked to a 12-inch leader wire, .022 for Mackerel. Then place a good swivel between leader and line.

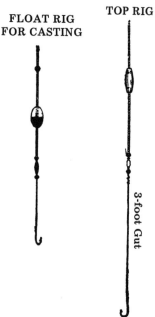

FLOAT RIG FOR CASTING

TOP RIG

3-foot Gut

PLUG AND TRAILER

The Plug and Trailer Rig, used mostly for Sea Trout, is very effective. Many fishermen use this rig constantly, and swear by it.

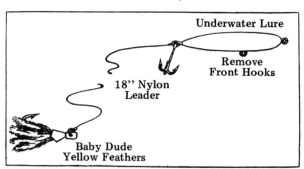

Underwater Lure

Remove Front Hooks

18" Nylon Leader

Baby Dude Yellow Feathers

The idea is to fool a fish into believing a helpless and tender baby fish is trailing its mother and is easy prey for the "big bad wolf" gamefish.

Rigging Method: Take an underwater plug (most any kind will do), that retrieves a foot or so below the surface. Remove the front hooks. Fasten a 12-inch piece of nylon leader to the tail hook eye. To this fasten a small feather lure of yellow color.

The rig can be trolled at about 2 miles an hour, or cast and retrieved with jerks, not too violent. Just reeling it in will bring results.

For Spotted Sea Trout it is the best rig — especially when the Trout are not striking hard. The small lure and hook gets them more often than a larger one.

Crab Pot Construction

CHESAPEAKE BAY TYPE

By Emmett Andrews, Division of Commercial Fisheries

The crab pot represents the latest in a rather long line of ingenious devices for catching crabs, some of which have been patented. Its construction is very simple and the materials are relatively inexpensive. It, too, has advantages in that little attention is required other than a few minutes needed to take out the crabs and rebait it, although it remains in continuous operation. Bait such as menhaden or alewives is readily available, in most cases from the trap fishermen. Quite often, the pot will catch its own bait and help control predators.

Briefly, it is cubical in shape, each surface being 24 inches square. The material in the body of the pot is commercial grade, 1½ inch mesh, doubly galvanized, No. 18 gauge chicken wire. This size mesh will be more selective in the size of crabs taken. The lower funnels, usually one on each side, are made of 1-inch mesh for greater stability. Pots made of 1-inch mesh throughout will be found effective in catching large eels as well as crabs.

Crabs attracted by the bait enter the lower chamber, find themselves thwarted in reaching the bait by the wire mesh, move into the upper chamber through a second set of funnels, and find it difficult to escape.

Traps are usually set individually in a long line or in a series of short lines parallel to each other, about 100 feet apart, in water varying from 1 to 10 fathoms in depth. Fishing is usually done by a two-man crew in a 35-40-foot boat, but can be accomplished by one man.

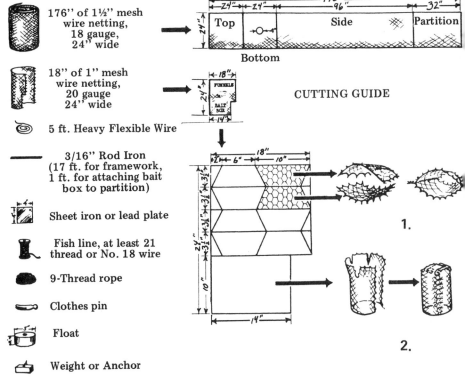

176'' of 1½'' mesh wire netting, 18 gauge, 24'' wide

18'' of 1'' mesh wire netting, 20 gauge, 24'' wide

5 ft. Heavy Flexible Wire

3/16'' Rod Iron (17 ft. for framework, 1 ft. for attaching bait box to partition)

Sheet iron or lead plate

Fish line, at least 21 thread or No. 18 wire

9-Thread rope

Clothes pin

Float

Weight or Anchor

CUTTING GUIDE

1.

2.

CRAB POT CONSTRUCTION

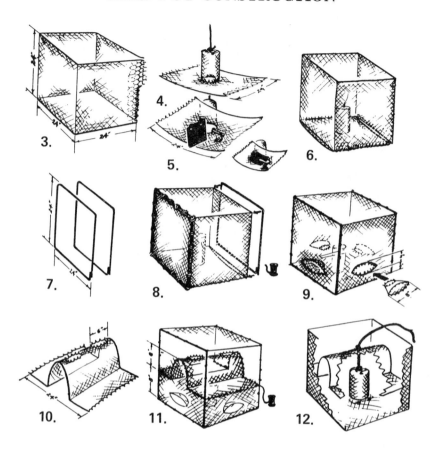

1. Make funnels by twisting together the edges of two pieces of netting along the short edges.
2. Make bait box by rolling strip of netting into a cylinder. Fasten by bending the wires along the vertical seam. Slash the top of the cylinder in three places, to make four tabs at the top, about three inches deep. Bend these down over each other to close the top of the cylinder.
3. Make sides of the pot by bending a piece of netting 24" x 96" into a square. Twist the cut edges of the netting together to fasten along the vertical seam.
4. Make bottom of pot from piece of netting 24" square, with a hole in the center 4" in diameter. Attach bait box to this hole by twisting the wire together along the junction. Tie 3 feet of 9-thread rope to the top of the box.
5. Attach 4" x 4" plate to the bottom of bait box. Make two wire hinges on one side, and use a clothes pin for the catch on the opposite side. Tie clothes pin to the netting, leaving enough play to let it slip over edge of plate.
6. Attach bottom section to the sides by twisting the netting together along the two cut edges with projecting prongs.
7. Bend 3/16" rod iron into two squares, 24" to a side.
8. Lash these iron squares to two opposite sides of the pot. Use either wire or fishline. At the same time, catch in the unattached sides of the bottom section so that it is now securely attached to the sides.

CRAB POT CONSTRUCTION

9. Cut four holes, one on each side, 2" from the bottom. These should be oval in shape. Attach funnels, small end in, twisting cut edges of wire together.
10. Make partition by bending piece of netting 32" x 24" into an arch, giving a final outside dimension of 24" x 24". Cut two slits in the top of the arch, 6" long, and bend the wires back and up.
11. Insert partition. The lowest part should be about 8" from the floor of the pot. Attach by bending wires on cut sides and lashing with wire or fishline along the straight edges of the netting.
12. Bring rope from bait box up through partition, and tie on an 8" piece of rod iron which is then woven into the mesh at the top of the arch.
13. Attach top, a piece of netting 34" square, to the sides on three sides, bending the wires together on two of them and lashing with wire or fishline on the other. Leave one side of the top piece which has straight edge. Reinforce the edges of this opening with a piece of heavy, flexible wire, weaving it into the mesh across the edge of the top and back along the upper edge of the side. Tie rope from bait box to center of top and tie another knot at the end of the rope. This serves as a handle.
14. Make a catch from a 10" piece of heavy, flexible wire. Twist one end around the mesh on the side, and weave the rest into the mesh of the top.
15. The finished crab pot, in position, requires the addition of a rope tied to the corner and attached first to a weight and then to a float.

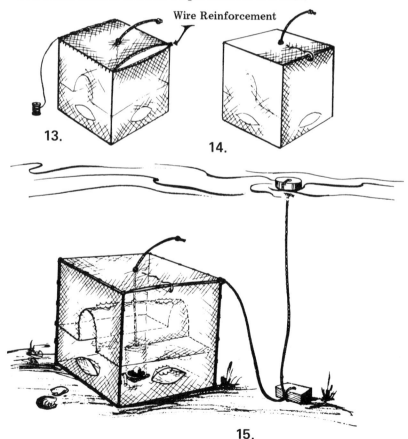

Wire Reinforcement

13.

14.

15.

Crabbing Essentials

YOU CAN catch Blue Crabs at the entrances of most salt-water bayous where there is a flow of brackish water. It's easy to catch them with a net attached to a long handle, obtainable at any sports store. Along the beaches, they come in at night, and an electric flashlight will show them up.

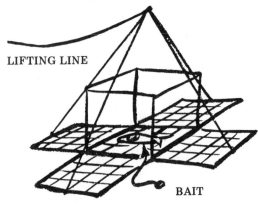

LIFTING LINE

BAIT

Many persons prefer the wire crab trap, which is lowered to the bottom on a line baited with a fish head or such fish bait. With a dozen of these traps lifted at intervals of half an hour, a good catch will be the result in productive waters.

Simplest crabbing is to merely attach a hunk of fish to a line and cast out. Let it lie on the bottom for a while and then haul in slowly. A long-handled net is necessary to dip up the crab hanging on this bait. He'll let go when you get him to the top of the water.

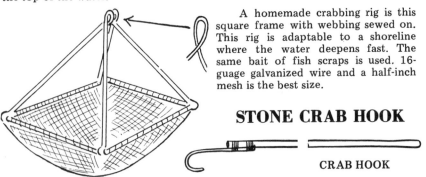

A homemade crabbing rig is this square frame with webbing sewed on. This rig is adaptable to a shoreline where the water deepens fast. The same bait of fish scraps is used. 16-guage galvanized wire and a half-inch mesh is the best size.

STONE CRAB HOOK

CRAB HOOK

Stone Crabs, most delicious of Florida shellfish, move into passes in Winter and dig themselves in along the edge of seagrass patches. On the days when a nippy nor'wester blows the tide, a hook such as pictured above will do the job. You punch it down the holes and, when something solid is felt, you turn the hook to catch the crab under the great claw, then pull him out. Watch out he doesn't get your finger in those claws!

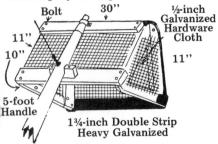

Bolt 30" ½-inch Galvanized Hardware Cloth
11"
10" 11"
5-foot Handle
1¾-inch Double Strip Heavy Galvanized

A handy device to catch Sea Fleas, Coquinas, or Fiddler Crabs is this scoop, easily made out of galvanized wire cloth and a hardwood frame. Dragging it in the surf will take the little Clams — and Sea Fleas, bait for Pompano. On the shore at low tide, you can tramp around a colony of Fiddler Crabs and, when they bunch up, scoop up as many as you wish. Also handy on most any kind of crabbing expedition.

Lobster Pot Fishing Gear

THE EARLY gear used to catch lobsters on the northeast coast of the United States was the hoop-net. This was made by fastening webbing to a hoop about 36 inches in diameter so as to form a bag approximately 18 inches deep. A rigid cross bridle was fixed to the hoop and, at the center of the bridle, the hauling line was fastened. The bait was suspended from this same point.

As the lobsters were free to leave, the net had to be tended constantly. To lessen the amount of attention required, the fishermen soon devised traps that allowed the lobsters to enter but prevented their escape.

Being homemade, these traps or pots were fashioned from many different materials, and varied greatly in both size and design. However, the lobstermen have gradually settled on two types of pots as the most satisfactory — the Semicylindrical or "Half-Round," and the Rectangular. The construction of these is now more or less standardized, except for minor variations in the size of the trap and the number of entrances. In certain fishing localities, small lumber mills furnish materials cut to the lobstermen's specifications. Thoroughly seasoned oak, spruce, and hemlock are favored for lobster pot construction.

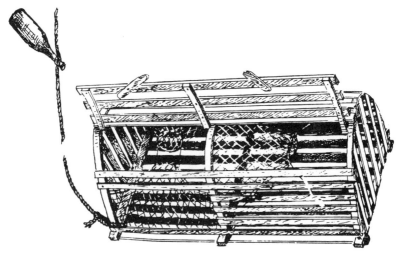

FIG. 1. SEMICYLINDRICAL OR "HALF-ROUND" LOBSTER POT

The Semicylindrical lobster pot found its first extensive use in Maine and, although made with varying dimensions and construction, is still the most popular trap in that state, as well as in some other areas along the coast. Fig. 1 and Fig. 2 illustrate the construction of a typical trap.

The base is about 32" long by 27" wide; the height is about 18" — all outside measurements. Each pot requires three bows. The bow is made from a board 47" long by 1-1/8" wide by 1/2" thick. Each end of this board is turned or whittled to form a cylindrical pin 2" long by 1/2" diameter. Three sills are made from boards 27" long by 1½" wide by 1" thick. Two holes, 1/2" in diameter, are drilled through each sill, centered 2½" from each end.

The board for the bow is steamed and bent to form a U, and the cylindrical ends are inserted into the holes in the sill so that the pins project 1" beyond the sill.

To complete the frame of the pot, two runners are made from boards 32" long by 1½" wide by 1" thick. Each runner is drilled with three holes 1/2" in diameter to receive the projecting pins of the bows. Two of the holes are centered 3/4" from each end of the runner; the third is centered 15¼" from one

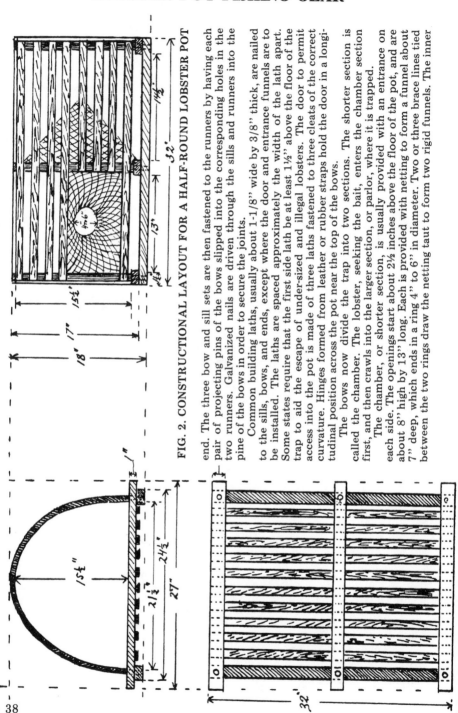

FIG. 2. CONSTRUCTIONAL LAYOUT FOR A HALF-ROUND LOBSTER POT

end. The three bow and sill sets are then fastened to the runners by having each pair of projecting pins of the bows slipped into the corresponding holes in the two runners. Galvanized nails are driven through the sills and runners into the pine of the bows in order to secure the joints.

Common building laths, usually about 1-1/8" wide by 3/8" thick, are nailed to the sills, bows, and ends, except where the door and entrance funnels are to be installed. The laths are spaced approximately the width of the lath apart. Some states require that the first side lath be at least 1½" above the floor of the trap to aid the escape of under-sized and illegal lobsters. The door to permit access into the pot is made of three laths fastened to three cleats of the correct curvature. Hinges formed from leather or rubber straps hold the door in a longitudinal position across the pot near the top of the bows.

The bows now divide the trap into two sections. The shorter section is called the chamber. The lobster, seeking the bait, enters the chamber section first, and then crawls into the larger section, or parlor, where it is trapped.

The chamber, or shorter section, is usually provided with an entrance on each side. The openings start about 2½ inches above the floor of the pot, and are about 8" high by 13" long. Each is provided with netting to form a funnel about 7" deep, which ends in a ring 4" to 6" in diameter. Two or three brace lines tied between the two rings draw the netting taut to form two rigid funnels. The inner

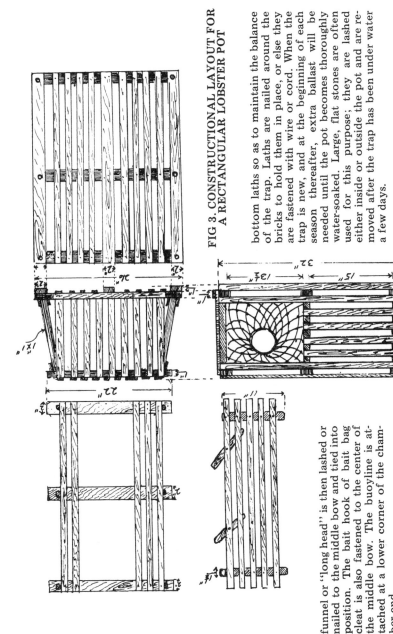

FIG 3. CONSTRUCTIONAL LAYOUT FOR A RECTANGULAR LOBSTER POT

bottom laths so as to maintain the balance of the trap. Laths are nailed around the bricks to hold them in place, or else they are fastened with wire or cord. When the trap is new, and at the beginning of each season thereafter, extra ballast will be needed until the pot becomes thoroughly water-soaked. Large, flat stones are often used for this purpose; they are lashed either inside or outside the pot and are removed after the trap has been under water a few days.

funnel or "long head" is then lashed or nailed to the middle bow and tied into position. The bait hook of bait bag cleat is also fastened to the center of the middle bow. The buoyline is attached at a lower corner of the chamber end.

The completed trap is weighted with 2 to 4 common building bricks which are distributed evenly on the

LOBSTER POT FISHING GEAR

The dimensions and construction of the half-round pots vary considerably. The pots may be from 28 to 48 inches long. In some localities, especially in Rhode Island and Long Island, the outer heads are often made of wooden laths wired together to form a funnel. A few pots even have the inside funnel replaced by a vertical, self-closing, lath door that traps the lobsters in the parlor. In other places, particularly in Maine, the bows are fashioned from spruce saplings smoothed and bent into shape.

The rectangular or "square" pot is of more recent design than the half-round type and is gaining in popularity. The absence of curved surfaces makes the rectangular traps more rugged and easier to repair. These traps also stack better so that more can be carried in a small boat or stored in a given space.

Originally the rectangular pot had only one entrance; this was at the end of the trap, and opened into the chamber, or shorter section. An inner funnel then separated the chamber from the parlor. However, seaweeds and other debris often caught on the buoy line and slid down to the lower corner of the chamber end, thus blocking the single entrance at the end of the trap. It is now the usual practice to build an entrance on each of the opposing sides of the chamber. With this construction it has been found that there is little chance that both entrances will be blocked by seaweeds or other obstructions.

The earliest rectangular pots were made of wooden dowel rods, 1/2" in diameter, drilled in a framework of boards. The runners were often fitted with steel shoes which took up most of the wear and also served as ballast. Many years of service could be obtained from one of these traps, but because of their greater cost and extra weight, relatively few could be fished by one man. Some of these dowel rod rectangular traps are still used by a few of the older fishermen. The present-day rectangular lobster pots vary in the details of their construction and range from 30 to 42 inches in length. A typical pot is illustrated in Figs. 3 and 4. It is 32 inches long and 15½ inches high; the width at the base is 26 inches and the width at the top is 22 inches, all outside measurements.

FIG. 4 — RECTANGULAR LOBSTER POT

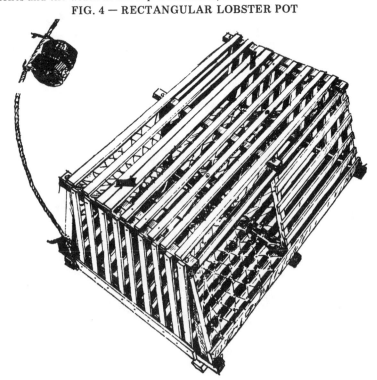

LOBSTER POT FISHING GEAR

In structure, the rectangular pot is similar to the half-round, except that the three bow and sill sets are replaced by three frames made from straight boards. The sides of each frame are 1x1-inch boards about 15½ inches long, the ends of which have been turned or whittled to form cylindrical pins 1/2" in diameter. The pin at the upper end is 1" long; the lower pin is 2" long. The top and bottom sills for each frame are 22 and 26 inches long respectively. These are made from stock 2" wide by 1" thick, in which approximately 1 inch from each end holes are drilled to receive the dowels of the sides. Since the sills are unequal in length, the sides of the frame slope, and either the holes or the pins must be cut on an angle. After the dowels of the sides are slipped into the holes in the sills, the frame is complete and the lower pins project about an inch beyond the lower sill. The protruding pins serve to fasten the frames to the runners.

Two boards, 32" long, made from the same stock as the sills, are used for runners. Three holes for receiving the dowels are drilled into each board. Two of the holes are drilled about 1" from each end of the runner; the 3rd hole 15" from one end. These holes should be bored either vertically or at an angle, depending on the construction of the pins.

The three frames are fastened to the runners by having each pair of projecting pins slipped into the corresponding holes in the two runners.

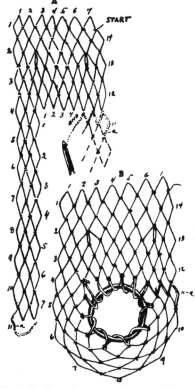

FIG. 5. Knitting Webbing used in Lobster Pot Head, 3¼-inch mesh. Outer (chamber) Head.

Galvanized nails are then driven through the sills and runners into the pins in order to secure the joints. A third runner, without holes, is nailed to the bottom sills between the other two runners. Laths, 1-1/8" wide by 3/8" thick, are nailed about the width of a lath apart to the sills and uprights, except where openings are provided for the door and entrance funnels. These openings are fitted in the same way as for the half-round pot, and the trap is weighted correspondingly.

With proper care, three or four years of service can be expected from either type of trap.

FUNNELS

The entrance funnels or head webbings are nearly always knitted by the fishermen or their families. A special heading twine of two-ply Manila or sisal fiber, 900- or 1200-foot size, is generally used when available. However, medium-laid cotton seine twine, 36 to 54 thread, is also finding wide application for this purpose. Jute twine of similar size has also been used with satisfactory results. The use of nylon twine is becoming very popular, especially along the New Jersey coast.

Since the heads are in sea water throughout the lobster season, they need to be protected from fouling and rotting. The fishermen apply net preservatives, such as copper oleate, copper naphthenate, coal tar, or water-gas tar to the knitted heads. These treatments materially lengthen the life of the netting. Sometimes pre-treated twine can be purchased.

LOBSTER POT FISHING GEAR

Figs. 5A, 6A, and 7A, respectively, show how the 3¼" mesh outer head, the 3" mesh outer head, and 3" mesh inner head (stretched measurement) are knitted in the shape of an inverted "L". Figs. 5B, 6B, and 7B show how the vertical leg is bent to fit the entrance ring. The dotted lines show the attachment of the vertical leg to the horizontal leg.

Fig. 5B also illustrates how the ring is fastened to the completed 3¼" mesh webbing by "mending." The double lines show the method of knotting the twine to form the half-meshes that hold the ring. However, in Fig. 6B, the completed 3" mesh webbing is fastened to the ring by lacing. The lace is finished with one knot which corresponds to the point marked "end" in Fig. 6A.

Metal or wooden rings, 4 to 6 inches in diameter, are used in the outer heads. However, as shown in Fig. 7B, the ring in the parlor head is made from a 6 or 9-thread rope which is reeved through the meshes and tied to form a circle about 4" in diameter. The finished parlor head is nailed or laced to the middle bow or frame. Two brace lines, tied from the sides of the ring to the bow or frame at the end of the parlor, draw the netting in to form a taut funnel and, at the same time, stretch the ring to an ellipse about 5 or 6 inches long. This narrow, horizontal opening, illustrated in Fig. 1, is flexible enough to permit easy entrance by the lobster, but makes its escape almost impossible.

BUOYS

The buoy line or pot warp is the thread rope connecting the lobster pot on the ocean bottom with the buoy floating at the surface. This rope is also used in hoisting the trap. These buoy lines must be able to resist continuous immersion and severe abrasion; therefore, when hard fibers such as Manilla or sisal are available, they are generally used. The fishermen buy the rope in coils and cut off the desired lengths. The service life of the lines is increased by preservative treat-

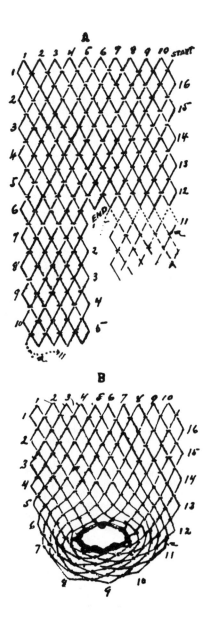

FIG. 6. Knitting webbing used in lobster pot head. 3" mesh. Outer (chamber) head.

LOBSTER POT FISHING GEAR

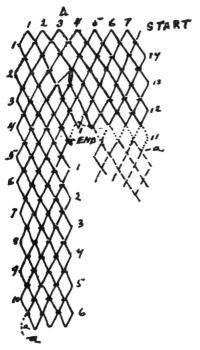

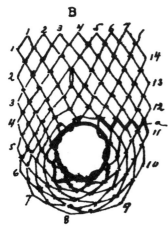

FIG. 7. Knitting webbing used in Lobster pot head, 3" mesh. Inner (parlor) head.

ments similar to those applied to head webbings. Cordage dealers often sell pretreated ropes prepared especially for lobstermen. However, many fishermen apply the preservative themselves.

When the traps are fished singly, the lobstermen use cable-laid 6- or 9-thread (¼ to 5/16" diameter) ropes. These are cut to be not less than a third longer than the depth at which the trap is set, so as to allow sufficient stray in ordinary tides or currents. For stronger currents, longer buoy lines are needed. A tightly-sealed, empty bottle or a cork float is attached to the pot-warp about 1 fathom from the pot to raise the line off the bottom and thus reduce abrasion and keep the line from catching on submerged objects. This practice also eliminates the possibility of seaweed sliding down the pot-warp and blocking a side entrance.

Traps are also fished trawl-fashion with as many as 30, but usually about 10, traps fastened to a trawl by means of 9- or 12-thread rope gangings. These are about 2 fathoms long and spaced from 5 to 10 fathoms apart. The trawl line is about where the current is strong; one end is buoyed and the other anchored.

Hardly any other piece of fishing equipment is made in so many colors and designs as the marker buoy. Practically every conceivable shape, from an efficient streamlined type to the modest "plug," in accordance with the fisherman's fancy, can be found in use along our eastern shore. Although there has been little attempt at standardization, buoys of streamlined shape have been found to float better in a current and to accumulate fewer marine growths.

The many color combinations and patterns serve as means of identification. Some states require each fisherman to have his particular color scheme recorded on his license. Two, and often three, colors are used; the upper part of the buoy usually being bright red, orange, yellow or white, for greater visibility, while the lower part is usually black.

Thoroughly dried wood that has been seasoned as long as possible should be used for buoy construction, and pieces that check or chack should be discarded. Cedar is extensively employed, but good quality white pine serves nearly as well. For long service and maintenance of buoyancy, the cells of the wood should be completely sealed by frequent, thorough painting. A minimum buoyancy of five or six pounds is necessary for supporting the ordinary 6- or 9-thread line. This can be simply tested by immersing the buoy with a 5-pound building brick attached. The depth at which the buoy floats determines its suitability.

BAIT

The bait used in lobster traps generally consists of low-priced fresh or salted fish, unmarketable species, trimmings from nearby canneries, spoiled fish, or fish frames from which the fillets have been removed. The cost of the bait is an important operating expense, since an average of 1½ pounds is required each time a trap is visited.

Oily fish — either fresh, salted, or partially decomposed — seem to possess the greatest attraction for the lobsters. Herring, mackerel, menhaden, and the heads of codfish lead the list as bait, but rosefish frames, alewives, sulpins, and flounders are in demand where they are obtainable. Lobster fishermen in some localities operate fish traps for catching cunners (sea perch) or other small fish to be used for bait.

When cunners or other small fish are used, or when the bait materials are soft or decomposed, they are chopped up and placed in small bait bags. These bags are knitted purses of one-inch mesh, stretched measure, and are treated with coal tar. They are suspended from the top of the middle bow so that they hang in the entrance of the parlor funnel. Large or more solid pieces, such as cod heads and rosefish frames, are placed on a hook suspended in the same position or on a wood or metal, barbed spear that rises vertically from the base of the middle frame.

FISHING METHODS

The United States lobster fishery extends from Maine to Maryland and to the southern tip of the Florida Keys, but the number of lobstermen and their catch is smaller to the south. The pots are set between the shoreline and the 30-fathom line, rarely deeper. Range bearings are taken for locating the gear. In most cases the pots are set singly about 10 to 25 fathoms apart; in a strong current, they are set the depth of the water apart to facilitate hauling. Where conditions are favorable, the pots are fished from trawl lines, usually about 10 to a line, spaced 5 to 10 fathoms apart. If rectangular pots are so used, they are usually made smaller in order to reduce the weight on the trawl.

The pots are visited and hauled daily during the slack tide, weather permitting. The catch is removed, the bait replenished, and the pot returned to the bottom. When the fisherman completes his day's hauling, the lobsters are taken to the shore station and placed in live cars. These are large, lath traps, the tops of which float just level with the ocean's surface and are provided with a trap door through which the lobsters can be removed by means of a dip net. These live cars are large enough to hold a week's catch and are constructed to allow free circulation of water so the lobsters are kept alive. The lobsters are held in the live car until enough have been accumulated for shipment to market.

Gasoline-powered boats, 14 to 25 feet long, are generally used in this fishery. In areas of abundance where many traps are used, two men often work in one boat; however, most lobstermen go out alone. Pots set in shallow water are sometimes tended in dories. If the distance requires it, these are towed by power boat.

REGULATIONS

As State fishery authorities revise their regulations occasionally, it is advisable to write for latest information before starting to fish for lobsters. Although state control does not usually extend beyond the three-mile limit, the lobsterman comes under state jurisdiction when he lands his catch.

HOW TO CUT BAIT

CUT BAIT is used for many types of fishing, often with yellow or red feather for Kingfish or Spanish Mackerel. Larger strips are used for Sailfish, Barracuda, Cobia or Grouper.

It is important to have bait fresh — and presented in most attractive form. Remember, the fresher, neater, and more appealing the bait, the better fish like it.

The illustrations show guide Buster Herzog cutting a Mullet for strip bait. In sequence, this operation starts with the top picture and is completed at the bottom.

Remember, fish are often more finicky than humans about their food. A neat job of cutting and trimming is essential. Loose bits of skin or flesh interfere with attractiveness and effectiveness.

You want the fish to get the hook as well as bait, so hide it carefully.

Let us proceed to cut up a bait: First, consider its use. If Barracuda fishing, leave scales on; they won't cut up the bait as quickly. This is important since the bait will last long enough after a first strike for another fish in the same school to attack. Most guides remove the scales for other fishing. This makes a flexible bait with realistic action.

Second, filet Mullet by cutting deeply behind gill cover and then slicing down backbone from head to tail. Cut filet into 3 or 4 strips as shown. The smallest strip (belly) is the right size for Kingfish or Mackerel. It is also the preferred piece because it is the whitest and most visible to the fish. The longer strips can be used as is (but with feather) for Sailfish, Barracuda, or Grouper. Grouper are often located by trolling slowly with strip bait. Once located, the bait presentation is not critical. Grouper will strike almost any meat put on a hook.

How to Bait the Hook

ATTACHING BAIT to a hook is sometimes the most important act of the fishing day. Fish, for the most part, are rather particular about how the bait is presented. Important point to remember is that fish like a live dinner.

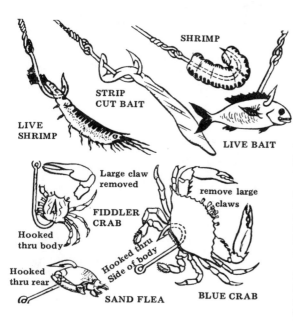

SHRIMP

STRIP
CUT BAIT

LIVE
SHRIMP

LIVE BAIT

Large claw
removed

FIDDLER
CRAB

remove large
claws

Hooked
thru body

Hooked
thru rear

Hooked thru
Side of body

SAND FLEA

BLUE CRAB

Shrimp, fished on the bottom or from docks, should be hooked lightly through the tail so as not to kill them, but to allow movement.

A strip bait or cut bait fished on the bottom should be in such shape so that when moved it will resemble a fish.

Dead Shrimp, beheaded, fished for small Panfish, is best threaded on the hook.

Crabs and Fiddlers should always be hooked from the back side. This allows the forward side of the Crab to be more lifelike and what a fish might expect.

Sand Fleas are hooked through the rear of the shell. As a bait for Pompano, they have some freedom of motion, which will do more to attract the fish.

Live Shiners or Grunts, fished for Tarpon, Cobia, and other top-water game fish are usually hooked lightly through the back at the forward edge of the dorsal fin.

THESE BAITS ARE GOOD FOR FLOUNDER

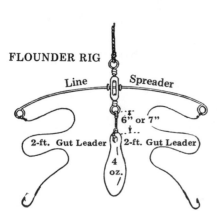

FLOUNDER RIG

Line   Spreader

6" or 7"

2-ft. Gut Leader   2-ft. Gut Leader

4
oz.

An excellent rig for Flounders is made by using a spreader. This can be purchased in most tackle stores. The principle is to have a heavy weight that will anchor the assembly in a strong tide so the two leaders, hooks and bait will play out with the current. Nylon is best for leaders, and Carlisle hooks, size 6, offer good strength and have shank enough to attach the bait. Cut Sardines are the favorite. This bait is not available all year, so live Shrimp or cut Squid will do as substitutes.

How to Bait With Shrimp

SHRIMP is far and away the most popular bait, wherever it is obtainable. Every animal likes this seafood, including fish, birds, and humans. There is hardly a body of water, fresh or salt, where Shrimp will not catch something when used

Do not put hook thru this dark spot

as bait. Fish, which are the best food for humans, are also more particular in their food; they like Shrimp alive. The proper presentation often means the difference between success and failure.

Opposite on this page is an illustration showing the best method of placing a live Shrimp on the hook. In each instance below, a particular method is used for certain fish. On the bays and rivers where water is 6 to 8 feet deep and a carpet of grass covers the bottom, Shrimp should be hooked lightly so that activity will be possible. This will lure the Trout.

Generally speaking, this method is considered best in most fishing areas. The idea is to hook the Shrimp where the least damage will occur — and have the hook where the fish will get it if he strikes for the head. Below on this page are three other methods — all good for situations described.

In the top left illustration, the hook is run through the fleshy part of the back, just behind the head. Notice the dark spot on the head; this should be avoided. A hook penetrating this area will kill the Shrimp instantly.

Hooked this way, the Shrimp can leap and maneuver, causing a Trout to lunge for it with wide open mouth — and take the hook.

In the top right illustration, another fishing situation is handled. Fishing for Whiting or Channel Bass, a Shrimp should be presented so as to resemble that which the fish is accustomed to seeing. This, we hook through the tail. As the bait is on the bottom, it is easier to work with the tide and move about with the line trailing behind. Bottom-feeding fish take a Shrimp head-first, thus bringing the hook into position for catching the fish's lip.

If the Shrimp is dead (lower illustration), a measure of life-action can be imparted by threading the hook underneath. The weight of the hook will pull the Shrimp down in an upright position, and give some appearance of life.

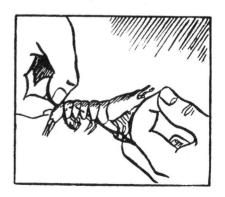

Using dead Shrimp when fish are biting well is often as profitable as using live Shrimp, if the line is kept active.

Eel and Squid

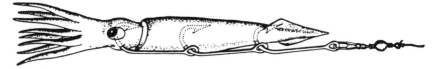

This is a good rig to use with fresh Squid. Using three hooks together, point and barb forced through eye, the Squid is strung on. A combination such as this is quite effective for surfacing Striped Bass.

A quick eel rig can be made without a needle and without the difficult job of sewing the bait on a hook. A few coils of twisted copper wire at the head of the eel holds a plumber's chain with three hooks attached. The whole is lashed to the eel's body with thread.

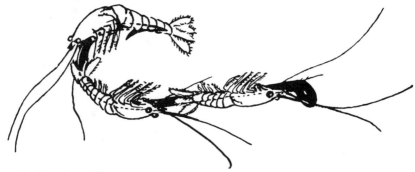

Quite often, Whiting or bottom-feeding fish such as Drum or Redfish, are taken in with a well-filled hook. Three small Shrimp can be threaded on, with the nose toward the eye. The last Shrimp has the point of the hook protruding from the belly.

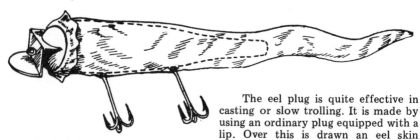

The eel plug is quite effective in casting or slow trolling. It is made by using an ordinary plug equipped with a lip. Over this is drawn an eel skin securely tied down on the forward end. Quite effective for all manner of surface fish, especially the Mackerel family.

Rigging Live Bait

WHEN FISHING on the bottom with a fishfinder rig, remember to hook the live bait in the throat instead of the back. Bait will swim toward the surface and the hook will hang underneath. Otherwise, the weight of the hook will cause the bait to turn belly up and become unattractive to gamefish.

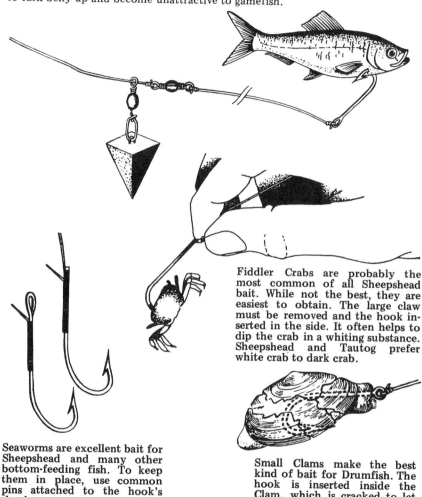

Fiddler Crabs are probably the most common of all Sheepshead bait. While not the best, they are easiest to obtain. The large claw must be removed and the hook inserted in the side. It often helps to dip the crab in a whiting substance. Sheepshead and Tautog prefer white crab to dark crab.

Seaworms are excellent bait for Sheepshead and many other bottom-feeding fish. To keep them in place, use common pins attached to the hook's shank.

Small Clams make the best kind of bait for Drumfish. The hook is inserted inside the Clam, which is cracked to let the juices escape just before it is cast out.

A bait high in efficiency and very attractive to Sheepshead and other crustacean-feeding fish is the Oyster. Small Oysters with tough membranes are best. In southern states these can be gathered at the roots of mangrove trees. Often the large barnacles on dock pilings do nicely. The idea is to fold the tough part of the Oyster over the fine point of a hook, small enough to be sucked into the mouth of a Pinfish. Fine leader of nylon is essential in the use of this bait — and best results are obtained by floating it in the vicinity of an object where barnacles grow.

Live Bait for Bass or Bream

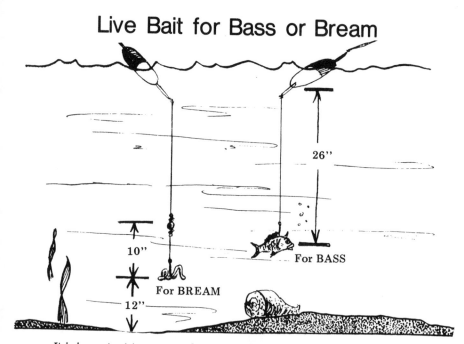

26"

For BASS

10"

For BREAM

12"

It is important to present the bait at correct depth for Bass or Bream

BASS WILL strike practically any bait found in the area where you intend to fish. Experiment with frogs, big grasshoppers, grubs, bonnet worms (to be found by splitting a bonnet stalk), tadpoles, and crawfish.

The Shiner is the stock-in-trade bait chosen by "live" fishermen at Florida fish-camps. The bait has accounted for more king-sized Bass than all others put together! The Shiner may be used in several different ways. Use a 3-0 No. 214 Eagle Claw hook and insert the hook from the lower lip up through the upper lip. This method is used for slow trolling and is deadly. Most Shiner fishing is done by using a cork or bobber and using a 1-0 or 2-0 hook No. 84 Eagle Claw. Insert the hook just forward of the dorsal fin.

You may catch your own by using a small hook and baiting with pieces of Shrimp or bits of worm.

A menu for Bass would read like this: Shiners, eels, frogs, worms, tadpoles, crickets, and grasshoppers. Goldfish are prohibited by law to be used as bait because, if they were to escape, they would multiply so rapidly, it would upset nature's balance.

BAIT FISH LURE

1½"

Balao or other bait fish can be caught with a lure more ofteh than with bait. Take an ordinary jig, pull the nylon hairs out and tie them with yellow thread to a No. 16 Kirby hook at the eye and near the bend. This lure works best when rubbed over the meat of Shrimp, Crawfish, or any type of shellfish that is handy. To complete the outfit, attach a light cane pole with 4-lb. test monofilament line.

Florida Warm Water Fishing

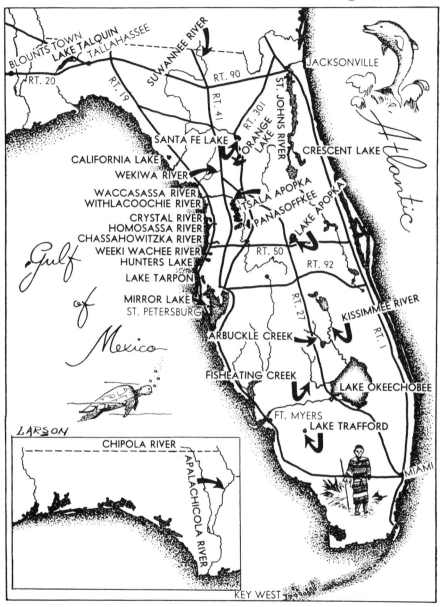

Florida is blessed with many spring-fed rivers which maintain a constant 72° of temperature. In the Winter, fish migrating in Gulf of Mexico waters, enter these rivers to enjoy a comfortable living temperature. As the natural food they are accustomed to in the Gulf is not available in the rivers, they become exceedingly hungry and, consequently, fishing during the months of November, December, and January is fantastic.

Where to Fish

ANALYZE the body of water you plan to fish. Look for the most likely spots which a fish would use for cover — weed beds, clumps of lily pads, brush piles, bars, and creek mouths. Fish a shoreline for a few minutes, then move on. Fish have tails and they use them! Just keep plugging until you have located the place where fish are biting.

Fish are fond of good cover. A shoreline heavily infested with weed growth is one of their choice hiding places. They hang around islands and heavy growths of lily pads.

The entrance of a small creek is an excellent place to toss your lure, as fish lie in wait for minnows and other food to float out of these small tributaries.

In many lakes you will find small clumps of weed growth consisting of flags and bonnets. These should be carefully gone over.

The bottom growth is generally heavy in clear rivers and streams, and the fish are deep down in the Manatee grass.

SWIFT RIVERS

Ease your boat into a bank and fish the eddies or counter-currents.

In any fast body of water, the eddies and lees are the best spots to fish. In certain constricted areas, the water around bends becomes the place to cast your lure. A good salt-water jig seems to work well in exceptionally fast water.

The majority of the Bass population leave swift-flowing streams and seek the quiet waters of the dead-end branches. Often, when the rivers are high from rainwater, they will overflow onto the flatlands. Fish will work and strike at minnows in shallow spots where the water drains into the deeper river.

When fishing the main body of a fast-flowing river, it is a good idea to ease your boat into the bank and hold it there by tying to tree limbs. Then make your casts into the eddies or counter-currents around the bends of the stream.

During the rainy periods, when normal sluggish rivers are running fast, the fisherman must take to still water in order to catch fish

Bass Fishing Methods

BOBBING FOR TROUT

Use a long and supple bamboo pole with about 4 feet of heavy, hard-laid snapper line tied to the end of the pole. On the other end of the line dangle a big spinner. A treble hook should lie almost invisible beneath the surrounding feather. Any fish that strikes will surely stay hooked.

Row slowly along the banks, just a long bobbing pole-length away. Flip the spinner near the bank and drag the bait over the surface. It sets up a terrific burbling sound as the blades rotate.

INNER TUBE FISHING

A novel way to enjoy a lazy, hot Summer day is to "inner-tube fish." First select a fair-sized inner tube and take it to your awning man or sailmaker. Have him measure your own back sides, and sew a seat from heavy canvas, putting holes for your legs to extend through. Fasten this to the tube by snaps.

A pair of rubber swim flippers will quietly propel your round craft at slow casting speed. If you fish a flowing river, dispense with the flippers and just drift.

Lures for Bass

THE JOHNSON SPOON

BASS just love to lurk in thick grass and lily pads. To get them out, a weedless lure is the only thing that will do the trick. The Johnson spoon may be cast into the thickest weed patch and will not hang up. When used with a piece of split pork rind or a pork chunk fashioned like a frog, it has exceptional appeal for the Largemouth. It may be worked very slowly or skittered over the surface, depending on how the Bass are striking.

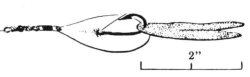

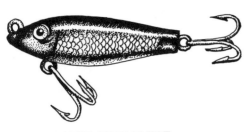

TOP WATER MIRROLURE

This little 2-hook top water plug is one of the best of the surface plugs for Bass. It is worked very slowly over the surface in a darting manner. With this plug it is best to use a spinning outfit.

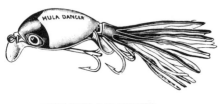

THE HULA DANCER

This lure is shown to give you an idea of the use of the rubber skirt that may be bought separately and used on other baits. The rubber skirt is a killer for Bass at times, and the combination of the Hula Dancer and the skirt is about tops in this type of lure.

THE SHIMMY WIGGLER

Of all the underwater baits ever used in Florida, this odd creation has probably caught more Bass than any other. With a piece of pork rind streaming from its hook, it has an action that is appealing to Largemouth Bass.

The inventor of the Shimmy Wiggler, Al Floss, had a fishing camp across the Chassahowitzka River and it is rumored that it was in the clear water of the famous old Chassahowitzka he developed this Bass-catching piece of hardware. The fishing guides around the river still stick to this lure and prefer the yellow bucktail to be used with it.

The spinner on the front part of the lure makes a gurgling sound and the bait may be worked fast or slow. At night the fast retrieve on top of the water is very effective.

THE SHIMMY WIGGLER

Wading to Catch Trout

OF ALL the devious ways and various methods of fishing, wading is a favorite method, especially if you're using a good fly rod and a floating bug. Select a sandy bottom and start with your favorite rig — casting, spinning, or fly rod. If you can get local knowledge on the type of bottom, so much the better. Muddy wading is no fun and extremely tiring.

Your old trout-waders with the felt-soled shoes are perfect for this type of fishing, but the typical Florida wader uses nothing but sneakers and shorts.

One item essential to this type of fishing is the angler's vest. It has zippered pockets, places for plug boxes, leather thongs to hold your rod while you light a cigarette or swat a deer fly, a detachable nylon creel that will hold quite a few Bass, a patch of sheepskin and wool to hold bass bugs, flies, etc.

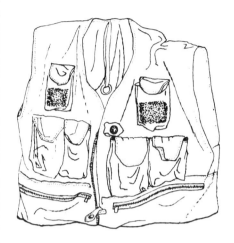

FISHING VEST FOR WADING

A useful gadget which could be a lifesaver is a tube of CO_2, called a "lifesaver pack" (about the size of a pack of cigarettes). A very ingenious little device that could be the means of saving your life. Made of plastic, it fits into a shirt pocket and is attached to clothing by a strip of plastic and a bulldog gripper. If you were suddenly to step into a hole or deep water, squeeze your pack in order to puncture the carbonic gas capsule, and you'll be quickly rewarded with a beautiful set of plastic water wings. These wings are capable of supporting 250 lbs.

If you don't go for the fancy fishing vest, you must have a plain fish stringer to carry your catch. Buy yourself a stringer with a loop on one end and a pointed brass rod on the other. Be sure to insert the rod from the lower jaw, to and through the top jaw of the fish. If you string the fish through the lower jaw only, some fish will gape and accumulate weeds and other debris. If you're fishing from a boat and changing spots, always sling your fish into the boat — the fast forward motion will quickly drown a towed fish.

------------ ✧ ------------

SNOOK PUDDLING

At night Snook are found around pilings of docks and bridges, especially in the early Winter when the chill is first on the water. A stout Burma pole with 12 to 14 inches of heavy line, a swivel, then a 12-inch wire leader, to which is fastened a plug, a white with red head is the "Puddler's rig."

To work this, you lean over the railing and drop the plug in the water. Whip it around in a figure 8 pattern so the phosphorescence is stirred up. If there is a Snook lurking about, he usually darts out and smashes the plug. Thousands of Snook are caught this way every year.

Fresh Water Rigs

IT MAKES a difference how deep you fish Bream and Bass live bait, especially Bream. The fishing can be good or bad according to how you present the bait. Bass especially are sensitive to the presence of objects such as corks and swivels. So, to get the maximum deceptive quality in your rig, keep the bait away from surface commotion.

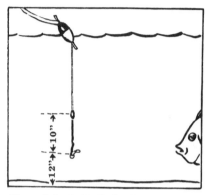

Above is best depth for Bream. There should be about 10 inches of line between weight and hook. The bait should dangle about 12 inches off the bottom.

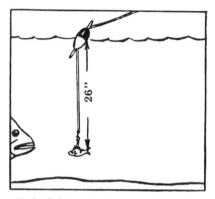

Cork fishing for Bass is best when there is 26 inches between cork and bait. Nylon leader, very fine, is excellent, although most fishermen tie line to hook using no leader material whatsoever.

MULTIPLE FLOAT FISHING

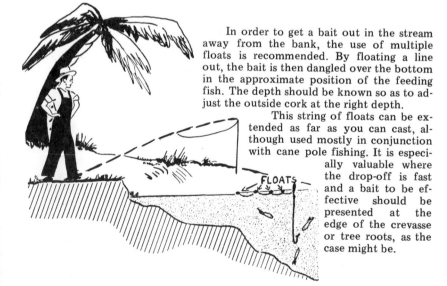

In order to get a bait out in the stream away from the bank, the use of multiple floats is recommended. By floating a line out, the bait is then dangled over the bottom in the approximate position of the feeding fish. The depth should be known so as to adjust the outside cork at the right depth.

This string of floats can be extended as far as you can cast, although used mostly in conjunction with cane pole fishing. It is especially valuable where the drop-off is fast and a bait to be effective should be presented at the edge of the crevasse or tree roots, as the case might be.

FLOATS

Tips for Bass Fishermen

FISH IN EARLY MORNING

BASS are early risers. Best fishing, if averaged over a period of years, would clearly show that the eerie hour of dawn is the magic hour, and second best, the twilight hour. Subdued light is better for Bass fishing.

In casting along a bank it is better to cast into the sun. Bass seem to prefer the shady side of the bank, and your lure and line, if cast so as not to throw a shadow, will get more strikes for you. By all means remain seated while casting. Your additional height when standing tends to spook the fish.

DROP ANCHOR SILENTLY

If you plan to anchor and fish, be sure the anchor is lowered gently to the bottom. Nothing causes fish to scurry away faster than an anchor thrown into the water with a big splash and a resultant thud on the bottom.

An aluminum boat is a fine piece of equipment for ease of launching and handling, but it is noisy. Any movement in the boat will cause a metallic sound that is a Bass-spooker for sure!

USE A BRANCH TO GET ACTION

Sometimes your lure will be cast over a limb or some other projection. Give slack and let your plug settle to the water once; then crank a few turns on your reel and dangle the bait a few inches from the water. Let it dance from the action of your rod. Surprising how many times this will entice a Bass to come out of the water for your bait.

If you should happen to cast your lure over a limb that is too high to reach, give your line slack to lower the lure, break it off, reel in your line, and re-tie.

Tips for Bass Fishermen

CAST FOR DISTANCE

Bass spook easily in shallow water, so when using a fly rod, make the casts as far as you can reach — at least 50 ft. out. You'll get a lot of strikes not expected. Long casts are preferable in the clear waters of some of our rivers.

KEEP PLUGS IN TACKLE BOX

When fishing, it is best to always place the plugs you have removed from your line in the tackle box. Did you ever sit on one?

Never leave the dock without a pair of cutting pliers as part of your equipment. The law of averages may eventually catch up with you and you'll have your anatomy punctured!

MUDFISH TEETH ARE SHARP

During your Bass-fishing expeditions, you are certain to hook onto an unpleasant-looking fish found in our waters — the Mudfish or Bowfin, a living representative of a fossil family. The Mudfish has an air bladder that functions as a lung. This mean character is also a threat to the Bass population. Be careful when you remove the hook from his mouth — his teeth are sharp and the jaw is strong.

FLEA ROD FISHING

Have you ever tried flea rod fishing? A flea rod is a 5½-foot fly rod. When wading in areas restricted to shorter rods by reason of overhanging trees, it may be used with great success. Wade quietly and cast or flip the bug into little open pockets among the weeds and under the limbs. Not only is this fun, it's also productive!

USING A SPECIAL BREAM HOOK

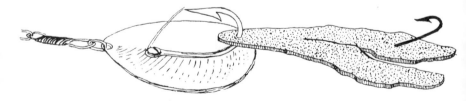

When Bluegills, Stumpknocker, or Speckled Perch are striking a pork rind bait and you would like a mess to take home, just insert a long-shanked bream hook into the pork rind. You will pick up the Small-mouthed Panfish.

Tips for Bass Fishermen

CASTING ON A LILY PAD

When fishing lily pads with a weedless lure, aim for a pad. If you have made a good cast, your lure should plop right on top of the pad. Let it rest there momentarily, then, with a slight twitch of the rod, ease the bait off the pad and allow it to sink to the bottom. With a quick jerk, bring the lure up from the bottom. This will stir up the mud and is sometimes very effective on large, lethargic Bass.

Continue to reel in the weedless lure with fast cranking of the reel handle, then let it sink momentarily.

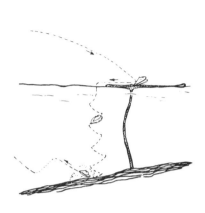

FAST RETRIEVING

If this doesn't incite the Bass to strike, then cast as far into the pads as you can and retrieve the lure at a fast pace, steering it around the pads and through the open places by working your rod. This is one of the great thrills of Bass fishing. The Bass can see the disturbance in the pads from a long distance away and will come charging through the stalks underwater, like a bull after a red flag.

CASTING NEAR DOCKS

Never miss an opportunity to cast your lure near a boathouse dock or any man-made structure in fresh water. Bass frequent these places.

A clean sandy bottom devoid of growth or debris should be considered devoid of Bass, with one exception: Bass will sometimes go to a clean bottom to bed and spawn. They will be extremely wary, however, when they are without a place to hide or without cover. When approaching this kind of spot, come up very carefully.

Salt Water Lures

IF YOU should set about to try every lure which would take fish in Florida waters, you could probably spend your entire life — and your lifetime income — and still have an incomplete collection.

On the other hand, you can stock up on a totally adequate assortment of lures at relatively little cost. The secret is to ignore the flashy colors and fancy promises of lures in general. They are mostly "fisherman catchers" anyway.

At the final analysis, it's the action that counts, and you can cover all the basic actions in something like a half-dozen baits.

Start with strong emphasis on jigs, which are the simplest, most inexpensive and most productive of all lures. A jig is nothing but a lead-headed hook wrapped with feathers, bucktail, nylon, or metal foil.

Any gamefish in salt water, from the tiniest Snapper to the heaviest Tuna, will strike a properly chosen and presented jig.

The selection of jigs is influenced by only two things — the depth of the water to be fished, and the approximate size of the fish you hope to catch. Consequently, if you stick pretty much to the same kind of fishing, you won't need much variety in jigs.

But if you fish the bay one week, the surf the next, and the reefs after that, then you will need a boxful of jigs to get you by.

For all-round casting, with either spinning or plug tackle, jigs from 1/4 to 5/8ths of an ounce in weight are the ticket. For fishing very shallow water, you might want a couple in 1/8th-ounce size.

Move out to deep, offshore water for Kingfish and similar species, and you will have to have more weight. From 1 to 2 ounces is the usual range here, but some anglers use as much as 3 ounces.

Even larger jigs are used for specialized purposes, such as trolling for big gamefish with heavy tackle.

Most popular colors are yellow, white, and red-white combinations. Nylon and bucktail run neck-and-neck as top choices of material.

Any jig will pay the most dividends if worked with sharp twitches of the rod tip. In general, overall speed of retrieve should be slow in coastal waters, much faster for deep-water fish.

A modest selection of plugs and a spoon or two will fill out your lure assortment nicely. Begin with two topwater plugs, a shallow runner, and a very deep runner.

One of the surface lures should be a cup-faced plug that pops loudly, while the other should be a darter type.

For shallow work, use the "actionless" plug, which you twitch through the water something like a jig.

For going way down, you'll need a lipped plug with a fast vibrating action. Such lures are often used in trolling for Snook, Tarpon, Redfish, and Kingfish.

This list doesn't even scratch the surface of the variety of plugs in common use, but if you master them, you'll catch fish under any condition you come across.

How to Weigh a Fish

IT'S A difficult matter to carry a device for weighing fish in one's tackle box, yet there are times when it is very interesting and important to know the weight of the catch. Whether it be to decide a wager or check on a world record catch, the weight of a fish is always interesting.

There is a simple formula which works well for all classes of fish of the usual variety. Thus, Tarpon, Snook, Trout, Channel Bass, and such. Fish with long tails or snouts, of course, do not figure out right if the measurement is taken at the tip of these extremities.

For instance, a Sawfish would be measured from the base of the saw or the extreme point of the head. A Nurse Shark with a long tail should be measured at the edge of the anal fin. Except for such deviations, the formula works well and can be used to weigh a fish with metal tape measure, which takes up no more space than a box of hooks.

Measure the fish from tip of nose to fork of tail, then around the fish just in front of the pectoral fins. Now take the girth measurement and square it, then multiply this by the length measurement and divide the sum total by 800. This will give the fish weight.

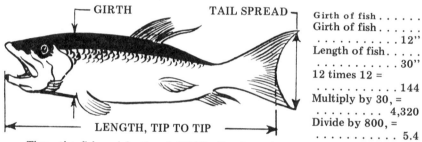

GIRTH   TAIL SPREAD

LENGTH, TIP TO TIP

Girth of fish . . . . . .
Girth of fish . . . . . .
. . . . 12"
Length of fish . . . . . .
. . . . 30"
12 times 12 =
. . . . 144
Multiply by 30, =
. . . . 4,320
Divide by 800, =
. . . . 5.4

Thus, the fish weighs 5 and 4/10ths lbs. A tenth of a pound equals approximately 1½ ounces, so the fish can be said to weigh 5 pounds, 6 ounces.

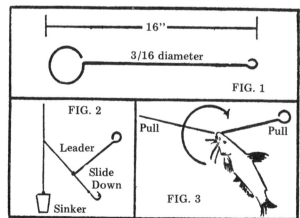

16"

3/16 diameter

FIG. 1

**GETTING
CATFISH OFF
THE HOOK**

FIG. 2

Leader

Pull   Pull

Slide
Down

Sinker

FIG. 3

About the most troublesome thing on a fishing trip is Catfish. To help this situation, here is a little gadget which will take them off. It is made of 3/16-inch bronze welding rod, overall length 16 inches. The loop in the end which slips over the line is left open so the de-hooker can slide down to the hook in the fish's mouth. With Catfish it works wonderfully. It is not even necessary to touch the fish at all! Just slip the gadget over the line and give the fish a flip.

How to Use Chum

FISHING, of course, is largely a matter of guesswork, and there are very few indisputable statements that can be applied to the sport. But there's no question about this one.

If you fish from an anchored boat, you're bound to catch more fish if you use chum.

Did you ever wake up in the morning and smell coffee brewing and bacon frying? Your nose twitches and your stomach starts doing flip-flops! You can't wait to get at it.

Chum has the same effect on fish. Oil seeps through the water, along with tiny bits of bait. The fish become aroused and hungry. They follow the chum stream. Little ones dart in. Big ones follow.

You can turn a seemingly dead spot into a very lively one by using chum.

A variety of chum systems are in use. Party boats, for instance, collect unwanted fish from the dock and grind them into mush. They take the mush with them in buckets and toss it over by the cupful to attract Kingfish and other varieties of fish for their customers.

Sometimes, when a party boat anchors, the mate takes a burlap bag of the ground fish and ties it to the anchor line. The stuff seeps out and keeps an automatic chum stream throughout the anchored period.

And the other common chum system for commercial or party fishing is to mix the mush with sand and form the resultant mixture into balls. This is just the ticket for deep fishing, say over reefs. Plain chum would drift away on the surface, but the sand balls have enough weight to get down where the fish are. It falls apart and the chum is released at a productive depth. Yellowtails, especially, are suckers for sandballing.

The methods named make too large a production, and too messy a one, for most small-boat sports fishermen. But they can be scaled down to a sportsman's level.

The angler, for instance, can replace those buckets of ground chum with a simple meat grinder. He attaches the grinder to the side of his boat, and when he wants to dispense chum, he simply runs a mullet or two through the grinder. As he fishes, he's bound to pick up some undesirable species which will give him a steady feed for his grinder.

As a party boat ties a chum bag to its anchor line, so the skiff man can punch some holes in a can of sardines and fix the can to his own line.

One last tip on chumming: Canned cat food (all fish) is available for a fair price in grocery stores. You can dip out spoonfuls of cat food and toss it over for chum, or you can use a beer opener to puncture it several times and drop it deep.

The idea of the whole thing is to get the fish in an eating mood. From there it's up to you and your rod!

How to Dress a Bass

STEP 1. Sharpen knife and rinse fish.

Fish in Florida waters have no superior in taste or quality, if they are prepared the right way. The way a fish is dressed makes all the difference between a fine dish of seafood and an ordinary meal.

Let it be remembered that fresh fish have no odor in cooking. A properly cleaned, fresh-caught fish sizzling in the pan could be a pork chop or beefsteak for all the fish odor that comes from it. If the fish is not fresh or has lain around after expiring, with viscera still inside — and perhaps been warmed up by the sun — there will be a strong fishy odor when cooked. The more pronounced the odor, the less desirable the fish is for food.

Take, for instance, Florida's kind of fresh-water gamefish, the Largemouth Black Bass. Some people say that Bass tastes muddy, strong, or is bony. Any of these things can be true, but it's not necessary. A Black Bass filet should be a piece of sweet white meat, with not a trace of bones at all.

The muddy or wild taste sometimes complained of comes from the skin and the abdominal cavity. The viscera should be removed carefully so that no organ is ruptured. The skin can be peeled off easily with the assistance of a sharp knife. Scales are left on the skin.

Here's the way to dress a fresh-water Bass, which is also applicable to all fresh-water sunfish and their salt-water opposites, the Channel Bass Striped Bass, and others.

STEP 2. Make initial incision along back-bone.

STEP 3. Slide knife along backbone.

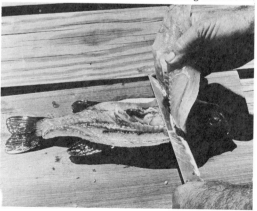

STEP 4. Cut vertically to backbone just behind pectoral fin.

STEP 1: Every trade has its tricks. An expert never attempts to dress a fish without first sharpening his knife. The honing stone shown in the center of photo is as necessary as the knife itself.

STEP 2: Lay out on a clean board with water handy to wash the fish. Starting at the head, make a light incision along the length of the backbone.

STEP 3: Slide knife along the backbone, cutting away the flesh. When the blade reaches the area where the rib bones join the backbone, cut thru bones.

STEP 4: Hold fish by pectoral fin and cut vertically to backbone at point just behind fin.

STEP 5. Cut filet free from backbone.

STEP 5: Slice carefully along backbone to lift filet free, being careful not to puncture any internal organs.

STEP 6: Cut filet free along belly line.

STEP 6. Cut filet free along belly line.

STEP 7: Remove skin by grasping tail and sliding knife along inner surface of hide with a sawing motion. Sawing motion is achieved by "wagging" the tail and working the knife simultaneously.

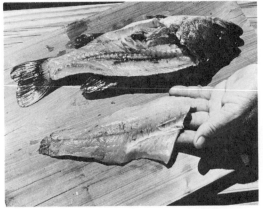

STEP 8: Remove rib bones by carefully slicing as shown in photograph.

STEP 9: Admire your handiwork. This method of fileting a fish is much preferred over older methods as it leaves the internal organs undisturbed — therefore, little likelihood of impairing the flavor of the filet.

FISH RECIPES

BAKED FISH

3 or 4 lbs. fish, dressed
1½ tsp. salt
4 tbsp. melted butter or other fat
3 slices bacon (optional)

Clean, wash, and dry fish. Rub inside and out with salt. Place fish in greased baking pan. Brush with melted fat and lay slices of bacon over top. Bake in moderate oven for 40-60 mins. or until fish flakes easily when tested with a fork. If fish seems dry while baking, baste occasionally with drippings or melted fat. Serves 6.

FRIED FISH

2 lbs. filets steaks or pan-dressed fish
1 tsp. salt
Dash pepper
1 egg
1 tbsp. milk or water
1 cup breadcrumbs, cracker crumbs, cornmeal or flour

Cut fish into serving-size portions. Sprinkle both sides with salt & pepper. Beat egg slightly and blend in the milk or water. Dip fish in egg and roll in crumbs. Place fish in a heavy frying pan which contains about 1/8-inch melted fat, hot but not smoking. Fry at moderate heat. When fish is brown on one side, turn carefully and brown the other side. Cooking time — about 10 mins., depending on thickness of fish. Drain on absorbent paper.
Serves 6.

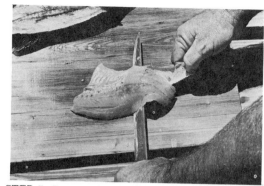

STEP 7. Remove skin with sawing and wagging motion.

STEP 8. Remove rib bones (optional step).

STEP 9. Heat skillet to 375°.

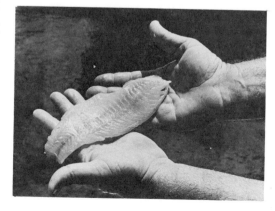

STEP 1: Take one fresh Grouper, one sharp knife, and one pair of pliers.

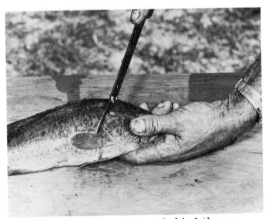

STEP 2: Start your cut just behind the pectoral fin.

STEP 3: Cut the skin completely around the filet.

How to Dress a Salt Water Fish

MOST POPULAR item on the menu of seafood delicacies is Grouper, usually referred to as "Sea Bass" in the fish markets. This fish, right on top as a desirable food fish, is more palatable if dressed correctly. Grouper is very much like fresh-water Bass. However, several anatomical differences make necessary a slightly changed technique in dressing. The following step-by-step instructions show a Grouper being made ready for a frying pan.

STEP 1: The fish and tools necessary for carving are at hand: a sharp knife and a pair of pliers or grippers to grasp the skin for stripping.

STEP 2: First cut is made just behind the pectoral fin, then down the back along the edge of the dorsal fin. Only the skin is cut along the top, but a deep cut to the backbone is made behind the pectoral fin.

STEP 3: Final cut is made along the belly, joining with the top cut and across the tail about 1" up from tail fin. This brings the skin free from the fish.

STEP 4: The skin is now grasped at the corner near the top of the head using a pair of pliers or grippers. A quick jerk will rip it off leaving the meat exposed.

STEP 5: A cut is now made around the head, under the bone at the edge of the gill cover, on both sides. This cuts out the Grouper 'throat' — choicest of the meat.

STEP 6: The knife edge, when slid along the backbone, cuts free a filet, boneless and pure white meat. The same operation for both sides.

STEP 4: Grasp skin as shown and pull free.

Preparing

the Fish

DEEP FAT FRIED FISH

2 lbs. filets, steaks or pan-dressed fish
1 tsp. salt
Dash pepper
1 egg
1 tbsp. milk or water
1 cup breadcrumbs, cracker crumbs, cornmeal, or flour

Cut fish into serving-size portions. Sprinkle both sides with salt & pepper. Beat egg slightly and blend in milk. Dip fish in egg and roll in crumbs. Use a deep kettle with a frying basket and enough fat to cover the fish, but do not have kettle more than half full of fat. Heat fat to 375°F. Place a layer of fish in frying basket and cook to an even golden brown, about 3 to 5 mins. Raise basket, remove fish, and drain on absorbent paper. Serves 6.

STEP 5: Cut out Grouper throat — the choicest piece.

STEP 6: Slice out filet along backbone. Lift free.

How to Open a Clam

STEP 1: This is a Florida quahog clam. A tough-looking and tough customer, but if handled right, will give up gracefully. Place on flat edge upon solid surface where hammer blows can be absorbed.

IN FISHING and eating circles, the subject of clam chowder always comes up, probably because so many sections of the country have native sons and daughters who believe their clams are the best.

Having selected the nearest clam bar, the next step is to rent a rowboat from the closest boat livery. Clamming equipment is a regulation pitchfork or stick with nails, or spear — anything that can be poked into the bay bottom.

On the area designated, at low tide, the clam hunter will wade in water less than knee deep, poking the pitchfork into the bottom as he goes. When a hard object is struck, reach down and feel it. It should be round and wrinkled to the touch. It's the hinge edge of the clam.

One clam is enough for two persons usually, or a large helping for one person. Six clams are more than a pint — about 10 clams to a quart.

Once the meat is removed and the black interior of the clam cut out, the balance is all meat and very good eating. To prepare this tasty bit of shellfish, there is a choice of half a hundred recipes. Everyone has a favorite.

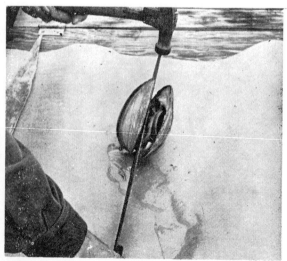

STEP 2: Take largest kitchen knife available. Insert edge in depression between closed lips. Holding handle firmly, strike knife short, sharp blows with hammer. Vibration will cause clam to relax, and knife will go through, cutting clam exactly in half.

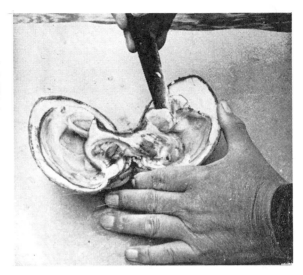

STEP 3: Using smaller knife, cut away the muscles on both shells. Then take out black center of clam, which is laid open. Cut in half.

There is no point in catching clams if you don't eat them, so that's just what we'll do now. First, we've got to pretty them up a bit. Clams, in the right kind of chowder, is a wonder to behold on the eating table.

In Florida, the tastiest clam chowder can be had at Fisherman's Wharf on Venice Bay. This may be disputed in other quarters, but your narrator thinks it is very good.

You may feel the same way after you have tried it. The best means to find out is to put the ingredients together yourself. This is the way it goes:

CLAM CHOWDER

1 cup diced white bacon
1 cup chopped onions
1 cup chopped celery
2 chopped green peppers
3 cloves garlic, diced
1 can of tomatoes, No. 2

2 diced potatoes
1 quart diced clams
Just a touch of: pepper,
Worcestershire sauce, Tobasco
Salt — be liberal with salt

Fry bacon and onion in medium-sized pot until brown. Add celery and bring to boil. Add peppers, garlic, tomatoes and puree — and bring to a boil again. Add potatoes; bring to boil again. Add clams and seasoning. Cook 20 mins. on medium to low heat. Add water as desired.

STEP 4: The entire meat of the clam can then be lifted out, after scraping it from the shell. Keep the shells lying flat to preserve liquor. Shells can be buried in sand for a week after clam is removed, then washed to become pearly ashtrays.

Cooking the Fish

Baked Grouper is an exciting dish.

OF ALL the fish in southern waters, the Grouper is the most representative species. Restaurants call this fish "Sea Bass."

The Florida Largemouth Bass is a close cousin — so close, that practical jokes have often been played on inland people by coastal fishermen, who drop them in lakes for amazing conversation.

The same procedure of cooking a Grouper will hold good for most any species. First, remember that this fish is skinned and fileted out, unless baked. If baked, the skin is well-scraped and scrubbed, otherwise a strong or muddy taste may infiltrate the finished product.

So we have a 7-lb. fish ready and we are going to bake it. This is the very best way to cook this fish. The next best is Grouper stew, which is a famous dish in itself.'. Here is what you'll need:

1 pkg. yellow rice	1 bay leaf
2 cups white wine	1/2 cup breadcrumbs
5 tbsp. butter	Pinch of thyme
Can sliced mushrooms	1 bunch young onions
Salt & pepper	

Taking the Grouper out of the oven.

First, wash the fish thoroughly with running water. Then lay on a board and remove scales. With a sharp knife slit belly and remove the innards, scraping all cavity lining out clean. Now cut off the head at the gills. Remove the gills and the eyes from the head. This will be done for you aboard the boat if you so request.

A 7 to 8-lb. fish is best. However, anything you can get in the oven is delicious. A good rule to go by is a pound to each person. A 7-lb. fish serves 8 people. The size makes a difference in cooking. You must cook the fish 1/2 hr. for each pound at 350°.

To start off, place the fish in a baking dish — best is an earthenware dish, such as the Cubans use. Sew the head back on and leave the fins and tail in place. Score the sides about four places, right and left. Rub a tablespoon of salt into the fish on both sides. Now dot with butter, especially where scored.

The rice is partially cooked as directed on the box. This is then stuffed in the cavity. Pimiento may be added for color and taste to the rice, if desired.

Mix the melted butter (2 tablespoons) with chopped mushrooms, chopped onions, and add condiments. Add enough white wine to aid in handling, then pour over the fish. Sprinkle with breadcrumbs.

Pour the wine in baking dish and put in oven with fish resting on belly, the rice forming a flat surface to support it. As the baking progresses, baste occasionally with the wine. Take out when brown and when flesh is still moist and flaky.

Serve on the baking plate surrounded with lemon slices and parsley. A good touch is to place a lemon in the Grouper's mouth. Now you've got a feast that's fit for King Neptune himself! It beats the barnyard or forest, and you will have to admit it's good.

Similar to all main dishes, Grouper has choice cuts. The throat is delicious — and the pieces of meat in the head are extra special. Third best is the cut below the backbone and above the anal fin (mid-section).

The strong backbone will hold the fish together and make carving a simple task. Using the scored points as sections, portions of the fish come right out in proper sizes.

There you have it. You just can't beat Grouper — and to those who talk about "Sea Bass," let them read this!